THE SCOPE OF CPA SERVICES

MODERN ACCOUNTING
PERSPECTIVES AND PRACTICE

Gary John Previts, Series Editor

PRACTICAL ACCOUNTING FOR LAWYERS
Robert O. Berger, Jr.

INDEPENDENT AUDITOR'S GUIDE TO OPERATIONAL
AUDITING
Dale L. Flesher and Stewart Siewert

AN ACCOUNTANT'S GUIDE TO COMPUTER SYSTEMS
William E. Perry

QUALITY CONTROL AND PEER REVIEW
James W. Pattillo

CPA LIABILITY
Jonathan Davies

EDP CONTROLS: A GUIDE FOR AUDITORS AND
ACCOUNTANTS
Martin B. Roberts

ACCOUNTING: HOW TO MEET THE CHALLENGES OF
RELEVANCE AND REGULATION
Eugene H. Flegm

THE SCOPE OF CPA SERVICES: A STUDY OF THE DEVELOPMENT
OF THE CONCEPT OF INDEPENDENCE AND THE PROFESSION'S
ROLE IN SOCIETY
Gary John Previts

THE SCOPE OF CPA SERVICES

A Study of the Development of the Concept of Independence and the Profession's Role in Society

Gary John Previts
Professor and Chairman
Department of Accountancy
Weatherhead School of Management
Case Western Reserve University
Cleveland, Ohio

A Ronald Press Publication
JOHN WILEY & SONS
New York • Chichester • Brisbane • Toronto • Singapore

A research grant from Arthur Andersen & Co. to support
this project is acknowledged

This publication is designed to provide accurate and
authoritative information in regard to the subject
matter covered. It is sold with the understanding that
the publisher is not engaged in rendering legal, accounting,
or other professional service. If legal advice or other
expert assistance is required, the services of a competent
professional person should be sought. *From a Declaration
of Principles jointly adopted by a Committee of the
American Bar Association and a Committee of Publishers.*

Library of Congress Cataloging-in-Publication Data:
Previts, Gary John.

   "A Ronald Press publication."
   Bibliography: p.
   1. Accounting—History   2. Accountants—Professional
ethics—History.   I. Title.

HF5611.P73 1985   657'.09   85-22455
ISBN 0-471-01149-5

Printed in the United States of America

10 9 8 7 6 5 4 3 2 1

To Mom and Dad—
and Matthew

Preface

This work might not have been undertaken, let alone completed, without the assistance of Harry T. Magill. He was of invaluable assistance in my acquiring an understanding of issues and in testing the realities of several of the historical propositions contained in this study.

Others also provided valuable assistance, most notably Kevin Head, as well as Brenda Wisniewski, Marilyn Murray, Suzanne Redmond, and Betty Tracy. Many professional associates in academe and practice assisted me in formulating ideas. I benefited from discussions with Andrew Barr, Charles Bowsher, Robert Mednick, Robert May, William D. Hall, William M. Hall, Herbert Miller, Victor E. Millar, Larry Parsons, Allyn R. Adams, Robert Sack, Richard Ratliff, Robert H. Parker, Robert Chatov, Theodore Barreaux, John L. Carey, and others. As the views and positions expressed are mine, I recognize that responding to criticism for any deficiencies must be my concern. Finally, I wish to acknowledge the support of Duane Kullberg, who recognized the importance of addressing the issues herein and respected the academic's right to follow the evidence to wherever it led.

GARY JOHN PREVITS

Rocky River, Ohio
October 3, 1985

Contents

List of Tables

THE SCOPE OF CPA SERVICES

Introduction

Professional men and women are accepted as highly skilled in some science or art, who desire to minister to other people, who want to serve the public, and who place service ahead of personal gain. If they were not regarded in this light, they would have no patients or clients. Who would engage a doctor, or a lawyer, or a certified public accountant who was known to put personal rewards ahead of service to his patient or client?[1]

John L. Carey, 1956

[1]John L. Carey, "Professional Ethics and the Public Interest," *The Journal of Accountancy*, November, 1956, p. 38.

1

A profession, serving the vital needs of mankind, considers its first ethical imperative to be altruistic service to the client, broadly conceived.[2]

The public accounting profession in the United States has been subjected to the same pressures from rapid social and economic changes as have other elements of our free, private enterprise system. The easy descriptive words for some of these changes, from "consumerism" to "regulatory reform," belie the profound undercurrents that indeed are shaping the way in which the business community, and with it public accounting, operates. Public accountants are being asked to undertake more and varied responsibilities for their clients, and questions are being raised regarding the propriety of their doing so while at the same time fulfilling their role as auditors of financial statements. It is the purpose of this study to trace the factors which underlie the development of the public accounting profession as it is today, and to identify issues requiring study in order to better identify the role of the CPA profession in a free, private enterprise system.

The term "certified public accountant" (CPA) identifies individuals licensed to pursue a designated profession. Not all CPAs are in public practice. Some hold positions in industry; some are in academe; others are in occupations totally unrelated to accounting. In varying degrees, however, all have an interest in—and a responsibility for—the vitality of the profession.

This study considers services by CPAs in public practice, the institutions and events that are backgrounds to such issues as the scope of practice, the range of consulting services, and competence and independence—all as they relate to the profession's duties and responsibilities to address the expec-

---

[2]Myron Samuel Lubell, "The Significance of Organizational Conflict on the Legislative Evolution of the Accounting Profession in the U.S.," Ph. D. dissertation, University of Maryland, 1980, p. 24.

tations of society. Competency and independence are among the most important traditional attributes of practitioners of the CPA profession. Maintaining these attributes through periods of vast technological, cultural, and economic evolution requires dedication, knowledge, and sophistication of all participants: the individual members of the profession, the leaders of the profession, corporate directors and managers, government officials, educators, shareholders, analysts, and the public.

Some significant concerns relating to achievement of the social and institutional rapport necessary to facilitate the proper attainment of professional responsibility include ignorance, avarice, indifference, and restrained competition. To some extent each element of society has responsibility to address these concerns; the key role, however, seems to fall to professionals and educators. What is finally at stake is the continued effective and fair operation of a private enterprise economy which acknowledges and encourages the rights and responsibilities of individual investors to control and direct the investment of private property as a means of productive capital investment.

A profession, its members properly trained and self-regulated, affords society a most efficient instrument of service to address the needs of a complex, information-oriented, international culture. What appears to be in question is the institutional size, structure, and operation of such a profession.

Since this study describes and identifies ideas as well as practices, it affords an opportunity to develop an understanding of the heritage of the CPA profession. A clear awareness of the origin and meaning of such traditions in practice affords members of our contemporary professional community an opportunity to benefit from the thinking of many individuals who have contributed to the literature of this subject over the nearly one hundred years since the CPA profession was initially established in the United States.

AN EXPANDING SCOPE OF SERVICES

At the start of the century, many professional leaders suggested that the ultimate domain of the CPA was limited only by the practice of law on one side and engineering on the other. Since that time the role of the CPA as business consultant, while not as widely recognized as the role of auditor and tax consultant, has emerged at an uneven pace, as the demands of a free enterprise economy have become clear.

The growth of the CPA profession (Table 1) has been steady, as evidenced by the membership of its professional body, the American Institute of Certified Public Accountants (AICPA). What is not so clear is the direction and nature of

Table 1. AICPA Membership Profile: 1887 to 1984

Year	Members	Year	Members
1887	26	1936	4,835[a]
1888	37	1940	5,437
1889	32	1945	8,964
1890	31	1950	16,061
1895	42	1955	26,345
1900	92	1960	37,897
1905	587	1965	53,709
1910	995	1970	74,413
1915	1,058	1975	112,494
1920	1,363	1980	161,319
1922	2,259[a]	1981	173,900
1925	4,047	1982	188,706
1930	4,815	1983	201,764
1935	4,515	1984	218,855

[a]For 1922 to 1936 the totals of American Society and American Institute are combined. These organizations merged in 1937. The organization's current name was adopted in 1957.

Source: AICPA Membership Reports

the services fueling this growth. In addition to auditing and accounting services, CPAs have provided tax and "other" consulting services. The dimensions of tax practice have been established by traditional accord, following protracted negotiations with the legal profession. The role of CPAs as tax consultants is therefore not a subject of this study. Debate over the definition and meaning of independence and the implication for management consulting services offered by the CPA profession has been going on for more than half a century. By the mid-1950s, a strategic opportunity to reemphasize consulting service to clients in addition to audit and tax became apparent due to increased demands on businesses, both large and small. Competition for consulting markets came from several groups, including members of the Association of Management Consulting Engineers (AMCE) and firms that had gained reputations as management consultants (e.g., Arthur D. Little, Inc., McKinsey & Co., and Booz-Allen & Hamilton, Inc.).

In early periods, non-CPA consultants tended to be more "proactive" in managing their service portfolios, relying on market surveys in deciding the range of services to offer. CPA consultants then were more "reactive," relying on the requests and needs of existing clients as the basis for introducing new services. Functional specializations of CPA firms later tended to manifest themselves depending upon the approach to introducing services—reactive or proactive.[3] Furthermore, in areas where computer systems design, implementation, and operation were concerned, the various groups (CPAs and others) tended to meet in head-on competition to provide services perceived to be expanding and lucrative. A February 25, 1985, *Wall Street Journal* article suggested, however, that "hiring a computer consultant can help, but the

---

[3]Gemma M. Welsch and James P. Ross, "The Consulting Profession: A Comparative Study of CPA and nonCPA Consulting Firms," proceedings of The Emerging Practice of Public Accounting Symposium, DePaul University, Chicago, Illinois, May 1983, p. 97.

field is full of incompetents."[4] Could the CPA profession
parlay its general and favorable reputation for competence
in tax and audit services into a "comparative advantage" in
computer and other forms of consulting?

Because CPAs held audit appointments and had become
acquainted with managements of public corporations, critics
expressed concern that, if awarded consulting contracts, CPAs
would be less apt to act in a disinterested manner in making
audit judgments. Also embedded in this contemporary scenario was the objection, often raised by competitors for consulting contracts, that an "unfair advantage" existed when
CPA firms as auditors also sought to bid on such engagements.

More and more frequently, however, the issue of independence was raised not only by competitors in the consulting
area but by thoughtful practitioners and by accounting
academics who sought an opportunity to contribute to the
discussion of issues from the perspective of individuals not
directly influenced by pecuniary self-interest.

SIGNIFICANT EPISODES

The development which impelled the expansion of the principal practice of CPAs (auditing) was the passage of the federal Securities Acts in the early 1930s. The financial community views auditing as the *raison d'être* of the accounting
profession, and the established state licensing procedures for
CPAs form a basis for social sanction over this professional
culture, controlling the franchise to conduct audits. At the
federal level, where the franchise is viewed as most lucrative
because of the Securities Acts, the legislation specifies that a
primary audit role be fulfilled by "independent public accountants"—where independence is now considered to be

---

[4]Michael W. Miller, "Hiring a Computer Consultant Can Help, But the Field Is Full
of Incompetents," *The Wall Street Journal*, February 25, 1985, p. 29.

behavior in accordance with professional standards as well as guidelines established by the Securities and Exchange Commission (SEC).

More recently, two other government actions have affected the practice of the CPA profession—the Federal Trade Commission directed the profession to repeal the competitive restraints which had been traditionally imposed on advertising and the soliciting of clients, and Congress passed the Foreign Corrupt Practices Act (1977). These have provided impetus for institutional responses by individual CPAs, practice units, and corporations. The responses indicate that traditional economic and educational patterns no longer are appropriate. If practice patterns, scope and range of services, and the nature of practice and client service units are changing, there is a need to educate all related constituencies: the public, press, educational institutions, and CPAs who are caught behind the "power curve" of such dynamic change.

AN ESSENTIAL POINT OF REFERENCE: INDEPENDENCE

The AICPA's second general standard of auditing states: "In all matters relating to the assignment, an independence in mental attitude is to be maintained by the auditor. . . ."[5]

Within its recently codified Financial Reporting Releases (FRR), the SEC stipulates, in FRR No. 1, that:

> The auditor must be free to decide questions against his client's interest if his independent professional judgment compels that result. If the auditor is predisposed or even appears predisposed, to blindly validate management's work rather than subjecting it to careful scrutiny, the ultimate result will be a

[5]American Institute of Certified Public Accountants, Statement on Auditing Standards No. 1, "Codification of Auditing Standards and Procedures," New York: AICPA, 1973, p. 8.

diminution of public confidence in the profession and the integrity of the securities market.[6]

One of the most challenging issues facing the profession is to develop and articulate an understanding of the complex concept of independence so that it can be of use in considerations about a strategic view of the scope of services by CPA professionals.

The concept of independence may be approached from a personal perspective as well as from a legal and regulatory one. Individual/ethical and regulatory/legal views abound, and substantial literature exists about each view. Independence is commonly held to be a "state of mind."[7] The view of independence considered herein suggests that independence *in fact* and independence *in appearance* are distinguishable. By viewing independence *in fact* as an issue of CPA "character" and independence *in appearance* as a matter of "reputation," a more coherent consideration can be given to problems at all levels.

OVERVIEW

In evaluating the issues and practices of the CPA profession relative to its auditing and consulting services, it is important not to expect "simple" solutions. In the final chapter specific recommendations are offered which suggest an agenda for the profession's consideration of the concerns related to independence and the range of consulting services offered by CPAs in public practice.

A key element in resolving controversies in a democracy

---

[6]U.S. Securities and Exchange Commission, Financial Reporting Release No. 1, "Codification of Financial Reporting Policies," *Securities Regulation & Law Report,* Special Supplement, Washington, D.C.: The Bureau of National Affairs, Inc., v. 14, no. 20, May 21, 1982, p. S–70.

[7]John L. Carey, *Professional Ethics of Public Accounting,* New York: AICPA, 1946, p. 7.

resides in the ability and duty of every interested group to develop arguments in support of its views and objectives in order to inform others. In this instance, the historical information presented, which is taken principally from the academic and professional literature of the accounting community, suggests that the debate is far from over.

The successive chapters in this study relate the development of professional practice during several time periods: (1) in the United Kingdom preceding the formation of the U.S. public accounting profession, (2) in the United States prior to the Securities Acts, (3) the early SEC period, (4) the post-World War II period, wherein a principal identification of the CPA was as an auditor, (5) the period of maturing audit services and expansion of consultancy, (6) the period of controversy, including a congressional study which created the label "the accounting establishment," and (7) the contemporary period, shaping a new identity for the CPA profession—for individuals as well as for firms.

1

Origins of Public Accountancy in the United Kingdom

DEVELOPMENT OF THE INDEPENDENT AUDIT FUNCTION

Sometimes one forgets how much he is indebted to history. It is encouraging to remember that those who have gone before set standards which the present generation can be proud to follow.[1]

E.A. Kracke

[1]E.A. Kracke, "Auditing Standards as Measures of the Auditor and His Procedures," *The Journal of Accountancy,* September 1946, p. 204.

Licensing of CPAs by the various states in the United States signaled the initiation of a unique approach to the social administration of the profession, one distinguished from its British counterpart. The American form of professional accountancy is founded on individual state licensure, whereas the British system is founded on chartered self-regulation. The subsequent overlay of federal securities legislation in the United States makes direct comparisons between the two systems awkward and perhaps even misleading beyond a point. However, to the extent that many common founders' aspirations were shared by the professional cultures, much in the American experience can be identified with that of British chartered accountants. One example is that among the 16 surnames retained in the "Big Eight" accountancy firms, five are English and five are Scottish.[2]

As will be seen, the concept of the *independent* auditor was slow to develop in the United Kingdom. Businessmen and legislators of the day at first held the view that an auditor would be most diligent if he had an economic interest (a stockholding) in an enterprise, thus, an incentive to protect his own property. This idea was consistent with an era in which owners managed and managers "owned" the enterprise. Only gradually—but with far-reaching implications for contemporary U.S. practice as ownership and management became separate functions—did the benefits of objectivity and impartiality provided by independence become clear. This development was a forerunner of the present notion of the wider responsibility of an auditor to parties outside the immediate corporate family. Today, public accountants, be they chartered accountants in the United Kingdom or certified public accountants in the United States, clearly assume that responsibility. In doing so, they support in significant measure the confidence in the fairness of financial reporting

---

[2]R.H. Parker, "The Development of the Accountancy Profession in Britain to 1919," unpublished manuscript, University of Exeter, August 1984, p. 1.

which underlies our respective systems of private enterprise. Today, the separation of ownership from management is accentuated by the existence of a professional management class, as well as professional auditors, analysts, and institutional investors.

It must be understood also that the first "auditors" were auditors *because* they were stockholders, not because of any professional expertise. It became the practice, however, for these stockholder-auditors to retain outside accountants with the necessary technical expertise to help them, thus providing the market demand for the placement of the audit function in the growing profession of public accountancy. Until that time, other and varied services provided a livelihood for "outside" accountants; auditing, so important today, was actually a latecomer on the scene. The desirability of seeking professional advice on all matters within the expertise of auditors, however, continued to be recognized.

As the various professional bodies were organized in the United Kingdom, chartered accountants began to develop the concept of self-discipline which is a hallmark of any profession. Some of the early leaders, for example, declined to serve on the boards of directors of their clients and otherwise began to act as independent consultants and not as employees or stockholders.

THE ORGANIZATION OF THE PROFESSION IN THE UNITED KINGDOM

Parker has identified important economic factors giving rise to the need for professional accountants in the United Kingdom:

> Four aspects of the 19th century British economy were particularly important for the development of accountancy: the growth of large scale organizations and in particular of the

railways; the development of the limited liability company; the high rate of insolvencies; and the introduction of income taxation.[3]

This environment and a predominantly *laissez faire* attitude toward business enterprise first bred the railway age and planted the seeds of the industrial revolution. This, in turn, spurred British investment in American enterprises after the 1860s and encouraged the migration of English accountants to American cities, as investors sought reliable means of gaining information as to the status of their interests.

Accountants practicing in the United Kingdom during this era found it useful to associate with one another in the city of their residence and practice. There came into being a number of institutes of accountants identified with cities, such as Edinburgh, Glasgow, Manchester, London, and others. The various city-based institutes were a natural outgrowth of the desires of their founders to form local associations responsive to local needs, including, most importantly, the needs of practitioners offering the same or similar services. Indeed, it was in part the diversity of those services that inhibited the later coalescing of the first organizations into larger ones of national scope. The United Kingdom and Ireland still have three separate institutes to serve Scotland and England, Wales, and Ireland (including both Northern Ireland and the Republic of Ireland).

In the long process leading to the present organization of chartered accountants in the United Kingdom, the question of the qualifications and services provided by those who should be admitted was crucial. Individuals not admitted for such reasons tended to form their own groups, leading to an increase in the number of organizations, the views of which ultimately had to be reconciled in the larger interest. One group, for example, opposed chartering because it made

[3]Parker, "Accountancy Profession in Britain," pp. 2–3.

stockbrokers and auctioneers, then entitled members of their group, ineligible for admission to the new association.

Ultimately, compromises were struck as to the occupations that were consistent with the practice of public accountancy and the conditions under which certain firms that combined with public accountants would not find themselves penalized. The reconciliatory phrase was, "further, no member who was not in practice as a public accountant at the date of the charter should follow any business or occupation other than that of a public accountant, or some business which in the opinion of the Council, was incidental thereto or consistent therewith."[4]

At the same time that professional accountants in the United Kingdom and the United States were becoming involved in the process of providing audit services, other opportunities for service were also being addressed. This suggests that the need to adapt to changing opportunities for service roles which related to the skills of accountants was an ongoing activity. Even so, agreement on what was an appropriate extension of service was not easily obtained.

Over the period of its development, the Institute of Chartered Accountants in England and Wales (ICAEW) encountered three principal difficulties in attempts to integrate the profession:

1. The failure to find any suitable or acceptable definition of "public accountant."
2. The need to decide the standards of qualification by training and examination required of a public accountant in order to protect the public adequately.
3. The problem of the "sitting tenant." This involves a decision as to how far individuals already in practice

[4]The Institute of Chartered Accountants in England and Wales, *The History of the Institute of Chartered Accountants in England & Wales and Its Founder Bodies 1870–1965*, London: Wm. Heinemann, 1966, p. 23.

in a specialized line of accounting, whether as qualified members of an existing body, or even as unqualified members, are to be allowed to extend their range of services and continue to come under the general umbrella as public accountants. Insofar as such practitioners were not qualified and members of a recognized professional body, the question of their supervision was also involved.[5]

The intellectual texture and composition of these three principal stumbling blocks should appear familiar to the CPA profession in the United States as it prepares to enter the twenty-first century. The problem of scope of services facing us today is not much different from the one that confronted early chartered accountants.

THE INTRODUCTION OF AUDITING: EARLY CONCEPTS OF INDEPENDENCE

Even before the formal organization of accountants into professional bodies, practitioners were developing their own expertise in various related fields. Important individual activities are suggested by the following description of services by James McClelland in a circular announcing the initiation of his practice in Scotland on March 12, 1824. Consider this partial list of services:

1.   Factor and trustee on sequestrated estates
2.   Trustee or factor for trustees of creditors
3.   Agent for bankruptcies

---

[5]The Institute of Chartered Accountants in England and Wales, *History of the Institute of Chartered Accountants*, pp. 150–151.

4. Principal in winding up of dissolved partnerships and the adjusting of partnership accounts

5. Keeping and balancing account books

6. Examining and adjusting disputed accounts

7. Making up statements, reports, and memorials of account books or . . . claims . . . before . . . courts

8. Looking after and recovering old debts and dividends from bankrupt estates

9. And all other departments of the accountant business[6]

McClelland, founder of one of the predecessor firms of Arthur Young in Great Britain, became the first president of the Glasgow Institute and was a prototype of the emerging accounting professional. By the end of the century, some 2700 chartered accountants served the British empire.[7]

Significantly, what is missing from McClelland's list is a reference to audit services. In historical perspective, the audit did not become a principal concern of the emerging profession until society, through its laws and the growing use of the limited company, created a market for such services. Much would change in the years between McClelland's first circular and the start of the twentieth century, including the predominant form of practice, education, and services offered by the public accounting professional.

By the second half of the nineteenth century, committees of auditors composed of shareholders and directors of limited liability companies were replaced by professional auditors in the United Kingdom.[8] Some impetus for this can be

---

[6]Richard Brown, *A History of Accounting and Accountants*, New York: Augustus M. Kelley, 1968, pp. 201–2.

[7]Tom Margerison, *The Making of a Profession*, London: The Institute of Chartered Accountants in England and Wales, 1980, p. 23.

[8]Ross L. Watts and Jerold L. Zimmerman, "The Markets for Independence and Independent Auditors," Working Paper Series No. GPB 80–10, Graduate School of Management, University of Rochester, Rochester, N.Y., March 1981, p. 22.

assigned to the impact of the 1845 Companies Clauses Con-
solidations Act provision (subsequently withdrawn) which
provided for the election of auditors from among the shareholders and *permitted the shareholders to employ public accountants
as their assistants.*

The sense of auditor involvement in the 1845 Act can be
determined by reading Section 102, which states

> Where no other qualification shall be prescribed by the special
> act, every auditor shall have at least one share in the under-
> taking; and he shall not hold any office in the company, nor
> be in any other manner interested in the concern except as a
> shareholder.[9]

Parker also reports that by the last two decades of the nineteenth century auditing came to replace bankruptcy as the
most important branch of work for most firms. Writing in
1921, Ernest Cooper (name bearer of Coopers & Lybrand)
recalled that:

> In 1864 (when Cooper started his career) . . . an accountant
> was regarded as associated with and dependent upon insol-
> vency. . . . People instead of using their capital entrust[ed] it
> to directors and instead of themselves examining the accounts
> employ[ed] auditors. But in the sixties professional auditors
> were the exception. Comparatively few large concerns . . .
> were audited by accountants.[10]

By means of example, Parker continues, the two auditors of
the Great Western Railway were a London merchant and a
Liverpool merchant—one later became a director of the com-

---

[9]R. Glen Berryman, "Auditor Independence: Its Historical Development and Some
Proposals for Research," *Contemporary Auditing Problems,* proceedings of the 1974
University of Kansas Symposium on Auditing Problems, ed. Howard F. Stettler,
p. 1.
[10]Parker, "Accountancy Profession in Britain," p. 18.

pany, both held very large amounts of property (i.e, stock) in the railway. The testimony of one of these auditors (Ques. 1920) before the Select Committee of the House of Lords, 1849, is instructive:

> One of the advantages of Auditors selected from those who are interested in the property is, that they may, if they see fit, reasonably institute an inquiry into the prudence and propriety of every charge; an Auditor appointed by the Government could have no right to apply any other than a mere technical audit; ... our Auditors have sometimes accompanied their audit with a letter of advice and suggestion on particular points.[11]

Thus also was cast an association between auditing and "advice and suggestion"—as early as auditing was established in modern corporate economic activity and while the accountant as auditor was only newly arrived on the scene.

The audit of this period was, again as characterized in the testimony (Ques. 1984) for the House of Lords, "between one shareholder and another; it professes to be nothing more than a careful examination by a public body into its own affairs."[12]

Not all reports about the audit system were favorable, however. An economic writer of the period summarized in rather grand fashion the entire business as follows:

> It is well known that on the presentation of each half-year's reports, auditors are appointed by the meeting of shareholders to examine and check the balance sheet. The witnesses produced before the House of Lords, consisting of public accountants, eminent railway directors, and others, distinguished by special knowledge of such subjects, were unani-

---

[11]Parker, "Accountancy Profession in Britain," p. 19.
[12]*Ibid.*

mous in declaring this system of audit destitute of all efficiency.[13]

One public accountant who testified before the Select Committee was William Quilter, who two decades later was to
become the first president (1870) of the "old" Institute of
Accountants. In response to a question (Ques. 2237) as to
whether he thought the present mode of audit (involving a
director or shareholder) could afford security for the public,
he replied:

> It never can in my opinion, and especially for this reason:
> that all the Companies make it a necessary qualification for
> Auditor that he should be a shareholder; the qualification
> should be that he should not be a shareholder, according to
> my notion; that is, he ought to be an independent individual,
> not interested in putting a favourable appearance upon the
> face of the accounts.[14]

Parker's study emphasized Quilter's testimony further as it
continued in response to a series of questions on the way he
carried out his work and the necessity for independence:

> (Q) 2218. "In going into those accounts, is your attention
> simply confined to the comparison of the entry and the voucher,
> or is the propriety and integrity of each transaction looked
> to, as well as the actual fact of whether a certain receipt had
> occurred, or a certain payment had taken place?"
> (A) "I should not only look at the vouchers, but I should weigh
> the probability of the transaction itself; that is to say, if it was
> an invoice, I should consider whether the thing was charged
> at a proper price."
> (Q) 2219. "If it was a payment, whether the payment was duly
> authorized?"

[13]Parker, "Accountancy Profession in Britain," p. 20.
[14]Parker, "Accountancy Profession in Britain," p. 22.

(A) "Yes; not merely whether it was made, but whether it ought to have been made."

(Q) 2221. "In those cases in which you are called upon by both parties, it is hardly necessary to ask you whether you enter upon those duties free and independent from any relative duty or obligation to one or another party?"

(A) "I should be unfit to enter upon the duties without I felt myself an independent man, not intending to show favour or affection to either party."

(Q) 2222. "When you have to examine into large mercantile accounts, it is presumed that they are brought before you in the shape in which they have been kept within the office of the firm, or the individual who has submitted them to you for his own satisfaction?"

(A) "Yes."

(Q) 2223. "Generally speaking, in large concerns, is there not some internal check established by the firm as a check upon its own transactions?"

(A) "There ought to be."

(Q) 2224. "Where such a check has been established, suppose the chief accountant, or the chief cashier, or whatever the name of the person may be who exercises the general superintendence over the accounts, to give a general vouchment for the fidelity of those transactions, should you feel yourself at liberty, when called upon to act in the manner you described, to take for granted, on account of that species of internal audit emanating from the parties themselves, that everything was correct and right?"

(A) "I should take nothing for granted."

(Q) 2228. "Therefore, in exercising your functions as you describe, it is not merely a dry arithmetical duty which you perform, but it is one involving the higher powers of judgment?"

(A) "Any audit, unless conducted in that way, might be done by a clerk, and as an audit would be of no value whatever; it would be rather a disadvantage than otherwise, because there would appear to have been an audit, when, in fact, there was none."

The Select Committee prepared Section VII of its Third Report to discuss an "improved and independent Audit":

> To render any Audit efficient, and entitled to public confidence, it must be freed, as far as possible, from all partial influences, or even the suspicion of any indirect motive; it should be rendered independent of those persons whose Accounts are submitted to its inspection.

Parker notes, "An independent auditor could be a professional auditor or a government auditor. The Committee called for the Railway Commission (a government agency) to be empowered to name an auditor to act in conjunction with the two shareholder-auditors appointed by the company. . . ." However, Parker concludes:

> The Select Committee's recommendations did not lead to any immediate legislation. The laissez-faire governments of the time believed that undertakings such as railways, which although privately owned had been granted many privileges, should be compulsorily audited (not the case for banks until 1879, or manufacturing companies until 1900) but were not prepared to require a professional or government audit. The Committee's recommendations were ignored until 1868, when further crises led to the legislation regulating railways and removal of the requirement for auditors to be shareholders.[15]

The rise of "modern" or professional auditing is best depicted in the fee schedules of Whinney, Smith and Whinney (Tables 2 and 3). Between 1860 and 1900—a 40-year period—audit fees rose from 2 percent of billings to 52 percent. Audit services in public accountancy had evolved, suggesting the need at least at first for some external specification of public corporate auditor duties, such as in the railway legislation mentioned previously. As chartered accountants' organizations developed and matured, they would assume the responsibility—as professionals—for such specifications.

[15]Parker, "Accountancy Profession in Britain," p. 23.

Table 2. Percentage of Composition of Whinney, Smith and Whinney's Fee Income: 1848 to 1900

Year	Insolvency %	£	Accounting %	£	Auditing %	£	Trustee & Executorship %	£	Special Work %	£	Total £
1848[a]	73.2	153	1.9	4			17.2	36	7.7	16	209
1849	74.6	600	8.2	66			11.9	96	5.2	42	804
1853	76.9	1,861	17.2	410			4.2	101	1.8	44	2,416
1854	69.4	2,488	27.0	970			1.3	45	2.1	76	3,579
1855	80.6	3,937	13.3	648			6.1	298			4,883
1858	93.2	13,478	6.2	1,091			0.6	106			14,675
1860	85.8	7,610	7.6	672	2.4	220	3.6	319	0.6	52	8,873
1865	93.9	22,814	3.3	808	1.1	255	1.6	387	0.04	10	24,274
1867	85.3	25,447	10.8	3,221	2.1	637	1.7	501	0.1	39	29,845
1870	96.6	17,751	2.4	451	2.2	413	1.7	329	0.07	14	18,958
1875					4.3	617					[b]
1880	72.3	9,965	11.2	1,544	10.9	1,506	3.5	478	2.2	297	13,790
1884	66.2	9,773	8.6	1,281	19.8	2,920	3.7	548	1.7	244	14,766
1885	60.0	7,420	8.7	1,073	26.0	3,217	4.6	573	0.7	84	12,367
1890	45.6	6,490	10.0	1,436	36.8	5,237	4.3	606	3.3	468	14,237
1895	15.1	1,464	22.7	2,193	54.3	5,244	2.1	204	5.7	549	9,654
1900	19.9	2,844	16.9	2,421	52.9	7,544	5.6	794	4.7	671	14,274

[a]Figures are for 6 months in 1848
[b]Only category positively identified

Source: Edgar Jones, *Accountancy and the British Economy 1840–1980: The Evolution of Ernst & Whinney*, London: B.T. Batsford, 1981, p. 47.

Table 3. Percentage of Composition of Whinney, Smith and Whinney's Fee Income: 1905 to 1960

Year	Insolvency %	£	Accounting %	£	Auditing %	£	Taxation %	£	Trustee & Executorship %	£	Governmental & Special Work %	£	Total £
1905	17.2	2,161	13.0	1,630	58.6	7,365	0.1	17	5.4	682	5.6	705	12,560
1910	53.0	15,010	3.9	1,091	35.4	10,018	0.6	158	3.4	953	3.8	1,087	28,317
1915	30.6	8,565	9.2	2,569	44.6	12,482	1.4	393	6.8	1,903	7.3	1,396	27,308
1918	31.4	8,542	7.7	2,091	48.1	13,078	2.5	685	1.8	499	8.4	2,273	27,168
1920	45.1	29,321	9.5	6,146	38.3	24,868	2.0	1,319	1.4	920	3.7	2,386	64,960
1925	26.8	20,449	8.0	6,123	48.5	37,093	4.9	3,719	7.4	5,633	4.5	3,421	76,438
1930	6.2	3,733	11.0	6,681	67.4	40,708	5.9	3,570	3.2	1,944	6.2	3,774	60,410
1935	1.9	891	16.0	7,531	67.2	31,614	6.0	2,831	2.3	1,078	6.5	3,078	47,023
1939	2.7	1,580	10.2	5,929	73.3	42,765	6.3	3,702	1.5	862	6.0	3,503	58,341
1941	3.7	1,820	8.1	3,949	73.9	35,922	6.2	3,026	1.7	806	6.4	3,112	48,635
1945	3.2	2,896	9.2	8,272	62.9	56,632	7.5	6,733	2.3	2,101	14.8	13,332	89,966
1950	4.3	6,577	7.4	11,272	63.8	97,284	11.2	17,040	1.4	2,129	12.0	18,298	152,600
1955	0.7	1,328	4.5	8,816	69.6	137,876	14.2	28,058	1.8	3,566	9.3	18,407	198,051
1960	0.2	736	8.4	29,006	59.7	206,025	11.0	38,009	2.4	8,384	18.1	62,784	344,944

Source: Edgar Jones, *Accountancy and the British Economy 1840–1980: The Evolution of Ernst & Whinney*, London: B.T. Batsford, 1981, p. 99.

Note as well that auditing was one of five areas—four specializations—which composed the firm's scope of service prior to the start of the twentieth century. From 1905 to 1960 (Table 3), the pattern completes itself in that insolvency work, once the mainstream of the firm, was now less than 1 percent. The roots of other major contemporary firms also can be traced to this early period. Another historian reports that the employment of William Deloitte to inspect the books of the Great Western Railway in 1849 caused a furor by the board of directors, who often took pains "to keep shareholders in the dark."[16] All of which suggests that disagreements between directors—those charged with giving direction to the capital—and shareholders were beginning to have some significance.

In 1864 Messrs. Deloitte & Co. were also appointed "the first and present auditors of the Powell Duffryn Company to effect an audit of the accounts" of said company.[17] And the minutes of the Telegraph Construction & Maintenance Co., Ltd. in 1864 note: "Resolved, that Messrs. Deloitte, Greenwood and Dever be appointed consulting accountants to the company." This was early evidence that, although auditing was on the rise in the profession, *consultation* was a designated professional function.[18]

The British Companies Acts established a sense of public accountability of investment in limited liability entities which were being incorporated at a rapid rate in the latter half of the nineteenth century. With passage of the Companies Act of 1862, the legislative audit requirement was temporarily ended. However, it had become an invariable practice for corporations to include an audit requirement in the articles

[16]Edgar Jones, *Accountancy and the British Economy 1840–1980: The Evolution of Ernst & Whinney*, London: B.T. Batsford, 1981, pp. 52–53.
[17]Deloitte, Plender, Griffiths & Co., *Deloitte & Co.: 1845–1956*, Oxford, England: University Press, 1958, p. 14.
[18]Deloitte, Plender, Griffiths & Co., *Deloitte & Co.*, p. 15.

of association, thereby establishing a customary basis for audits. In 1879, bank audits again became compulsory, and on the first day of the 20th century manufacturing companies became subject to a similar provision by way of Parliament's laying down certain forms of certificates and reports and providing that accounts of every corporation be examined and certified by an independent auditor appointed by the stockholders.[19]

AUDITING THE RAILWAYS

The Great Western Railway Company had been inaugurated in 1835 with a capital of £2,500,000. A professional accounting firm began a long and close association with the Great Western Railway in 1849, when the accounts, "audited" by two lay auditors, were also signed "W. W. Deloitte, Accountant." The circumstances leading to Deloitte's appointment reflected the need for an intermediary between shareholders and the management. A committee appointed in 1849 to consult with the board called "special attention to the existing system of auditing the accounts," and urged on the proprietors "the expediency of taking this subject into their earliest consideration, with a view to the adoption of an efficient, independent system of audit." As a result of the committee's inquiries, the question of audit was extensively referred to in the directors' report on the accounts for the half year to December 31, 1849, as follows:

> The auditors have been assisted, for the first time, throughout a laborious examination of all the books, accounts and documents of the Company, by a public accountant, whom they appointed without previous communication with any individ-

ual connected with the Company. . . . They have, by their signatures, authenticated the accounts, and have expressed their general commendation of the system itself, and the mode in which it is worked.[20]

The board also showed foresight by suggesting that what they had attempted to do should be made compulsory by the legislature:

> The directors must express an earnest desire . . . that some steps may be taken to secure the final adoption of an efficient and independent system by audit by a legislative measure during the present session. . . . Your board will therefore content itself with reiterating the general opinion that the audit should be scrutinising, continuous and complete, conducted by persons wholly unconnected with, and independent of, directors and officers, but possessing the confidence of the proprietors. The auditors . . . should be assisted by a public accountant, their remuneration should be fully adequate to their labours, but fixed in amount. . . . They should be required to report their opinions freely and unreservedly, as well to the directors during the audit, as to the proprietors after it shall have been completed.[21]

Auditors' duties and responsibilities subsequently were laid down by the Railway Companies Act of 1867. Railway accounts also were cast in statutory form in 1868.

PROFESSIONAL CARE, INDEPENDENCE, AND SELF-DISCIPLINE

Linkages between British mores and American business ethics became the subject of a lengthy editorial in the *Accountant* (Britain's major professional publication) on February 2, 1889.

---

[20]Deloitte, Plender, Griffiths & Co., *Deloitte & Co.,* pp. 17–18.
[21]Deloitte, Plender, Griffiths & Co., *Deloitte & Co.,* pp. 18–19.

A firm of British chartered accountants had refused to sign the accounts of a Montana gold mine. An editorial entitled "Independence of Auditors" detailed the difficulties encountered by British auditors as they attempted to represent shareholders against directors who delayed or suppressed information. Further, the editorial pointed out how easily a troublesome auditor could be "shelved." Chartered accountants were called on in the editorial to demonstrate etiquette appropriate to the gravity of the concerns such that the directors "ought to search the lists of chartered accountants in vain before finding a single member who will for the sake of a fee or a possible future audit, assist them in their struggle with existing auditors."[22]

All of this suggests that "independence" as envisioned by editorial writers of the *Accountant* required professional solidarity and self-restraint as a moral force in the face of a transgressing investment community, if the audit were to be upheld.

Earlier and similar episodes include a remark in a letter from Deloitte to a prospective audit client: "I regret that neither Mr. Dever nor I can see our way to joining the board." It had been the practice of the firm from the first that partners should not accept directorships of audit client companies.[23]

In more recent times following World War II, issues involving scope of services have led certain firms to reject estates practice (property management and rent collection) on the grounds of incompatibility of service. And a Big Eight firm is reported to have spun off a portion of its practice, involving investment counseling services to members of the English nobility, for similar reasons.

---

[22]"Independence for Auditors," *The Accountant*, February 2, 1889, reprinted in *The English View of Accountant's Duties and Responsibilities: 1881–1902*, ed. Michael Chatfield, New York: Arno, 1978, p. 53.

[23]Deloitte, Plender, Griffiths & Co., *Deloitte & Co.*, p. 56.

BRITISH PRECEDENT AND THE PROTOTYPE OF A MODERN ACCOUNTANT

As British chartered accountants were hired to audit British investments in the United States, precedents from the United Kingdom practice became points of reference in U.S. periodicals. Reporting on his survey regarding the dimensions of "the field of accountancy" in the July 1906 issue of *The Journal of Accountancy,* David Kinley was discovering that American accountants had found it useful to consider a speech given four and a half years earlier by a distinguished British emigre to the United States. He was a rapidly rising chartered accountant named Arthur Lowes Dickinson. Dickinson would soon be chosen to direct Price Waterhouse's operations in the United States.[24]

Dickinson's remarks had first been published in the *Accountant,* and were based on a speech given to the Illinois Association of Public Accountants in Chicago in 1902. Dickinson held that:

> A public accountant is not merely a bookkeeper, a statistician, or a man of figures, nor only a good man of businesss, but if he is to be successful in his profession he must combine all these qualifications and in addition have a general knowledge of all industrial undertakings, of the forms of accounting most suitable to each and of the general principles both legal and economical which govern them . . .

Dickinson concluded by noting:

> The largest industrial undertakings can, without legislation, do a great deal in this direction by the publication of complete statements of accounts, certified by public accountants appointd by the stockholders. . . . It may well be that legislation

---

[24]David Kinley, "The Field of Accountancy," *The Journal of Accountancy,* July 1906, p. 188.

will eventually be necessary before complete protections are assured to the public. But all those who are against government interference with private enterprises, while desiring to compel reasonable publicity in the affairs of commercial undertakings, can direct this legislation to safe channels by using their influence to so firmly establish the principle of *independent* audits by public accountants that the state will merely have to make compulsory a course of action already adopted by the majority of well-managed enterprises.[25] (Emphasis supplied.)

SUMMARY

Precedent-setting practice and debate in the British profession prior to the turn of the century provided a basis for several issues which American CPAs also addressed, as the industrial revolution and the corporate form of business became prevalent in the United States. Examples are to be found in specific passages of the testimony, cited earlier, in the House of Lords, given in the middle of the nineteenth century, to include:

1. A constructive benefit of an audit is related to being provided with "advice and suggestions" (Ques. 1920).
2. An *independent* individual not interested in putting a favorable appearance upon the face of the accounts is deemed a better candidate for auditor (Ques. 2237).
3. A recognition was afforded to the value of candor which could ensue from the involvement of a nongovernmental auditor and concern was expressed that an auditor appointed by the government would provide "a mere technical audit" (Ques. 1920 and 2228).

---

[25]Dickinson, "Duties and Responsibilities of the Public Accountant," pp. 153–60.

Finally, Dickinson and others forecast a public role for the independent auditor and predicted the legislative events which would establish the CPA profession's role in auditing upon passage of federal Securities Acts.

It would be unwise to rest too heavily on such evidence as supporting a particular interpretation of the term "independence" or the function of the audit. But it would also be unwise to ignore the import of such discussions. What is clear is the early and ongoing concern in the financial community over how professional accountants were to render services in a free enterprise economy in order to enable investors to evaluate performance while assisting managers responsible for achieving performance.

2

Early CPA Practice
In the United States

THE FREE MARKET PERIOD

A public accountant acknowledges no master but the public, and thus differs from the bookkeeper, whose acts and statements are dictated by his employers. A public accountant's certificate, though addressed to president or directors, is virtually made to the public, who are actually or prospectively stockholders. He should have ability, varied experience and undoubted integrity.[1]

Charles C. Reckitt, January 1900,
The Public Accountant *(Philadelphia)*

[1]Andrew Barr, "The Independent Accountant and the SEC," *The Journal of Accountancy,* October 1959, p. 32.

The early public accounting profession in the United States, along with its companion profession in the United Kingdom, depended heavily on nonaudit (or, as we would say today, "nonattest") services for its economic livelihood. But the growing importance of auditing in this period paralleled the growth of the public company and the increasing number and dispersion of its shareholders. Estimates of pre-World War I individual stock ownership range from 500,000 to 2 million; after the war, by 1929, the number was believed to be at least 10 million; although the information is not particularly reliable, the orders of magnitude may be.[2]

Even so, consulting and acting as a business advisor was considered a typical activity for public accountants. These professionals brought to the tasks a broad background and knowledge of business practices generally, as well as expertise in accounting and auditing. Early advice regarding the care with which these services should be provided so as to ensure that the real objectivity necessary to a professional performance would be maintained foreshadowed the distinction now made between the provision of advice and counsel and the assumption of management's responsibility for a decision in such matters. Nevertheless, the range of CPA services was perceived by many as limited only by the practice of the law on one hand and the field of engineering on the other. What is now broadly characterized as "management consulting" was initially within the province of the public accountant, but was also especially pursued by others who found therein a market opportunity.

By 1921 all of the original 48 states had passed CPA legislation, thus recognizing the status of public accountants and granting them a legal "franchise."[3] In the years between passage of the first CPA law in New York in 1896, and the federal

---

[2]New York Stock Exchange, *Marketplace: A Brief History of the New York Stock Exchange,* New York: New York Stock Exchange, 1982.
[3]Eric L. Kohler and Paul W. Pettengill, *Principles of Auditing,* Chicago: A.W. Shaw, 1927, p. 7.

securities laws in 1933 and 1934, which mandated the association of the independent public accountant with the financial statements of major publicly held companies, the American CPA profession grew into adolescence.

A.C. Littleton, a pioneer accounting historian and academic, pointed out that in the 1890s public accountants were frequently retained by promoters of corporate amalgamations and mergers to investigate the companies under consideration. Such financial investigations were a principal form of activity which he characterized as "audits for management." The evolution of "audits for stockholders," another form of practice by public accountants, was beginning to take shape by the start of the twentieth century, when corporations such as the newly formed U.S. Steel Corp. employed auditors to provide assurances about the numbers shaped in the ponderous ledgers.[4] In this arena the opinion of the experienced CPA was likened to a Good Housekeeping seal on a domestic product—and often it was conveyed in as few words as "audited and found correct."[5]

The *Journal of Accountancy,* the principal voice of the CPA profession, had been introduced in 1905. In its first issue appeared a somewhat prophetic article, "The Scope of Professional Accountancy," by Frederick Cleveland. Cleveland's article provides a useful view of the era. He asserted that administrative control was the province of the professional accountant—noting that auditing, and examinations made under special or general cases which relate to investor or creditor rights, were customary. He then stated:

> The general scope of (this) work . . . in relation to devising, installation and supervision of systems of control, in relation to auditing, in relation to the making of examinations and

[4]Kunio Chiyoda, "Error of Overestimating 'the Audit for Credit Purposes,' and Evolution of 'the Audit for Stockholders': From the Standpoint of Development of American Public Accounting Profession until the Year 1920," Research Study, Ritsumeikan University, Kyoto, Japan, September 1984.
[5]Gary John Previts and Barbara Dubis Merino, *A History of Accounting in America,* New York: Wiley, 1979, p. 178.

reports—either general or special—is well recognized and well established.

There are, however, he said:

> Certain aspects of professional employment that are not so thoroughly understood by the public. *Among these are the consultative and advisory relations with those who are practicing in allied business professions.*[6] (Emphasis supplied.)

In particular, Cleveland mentioned how the accountant should work with the engineer to ensure efficient and economic control in connection with machinery and how even more closely related the work of the accountant is to that of the lawyer, for example, in establishing the import of evidence in a proceeding which relates to the rights of an income bondholder coming to trial.

A few years later (1908), Dickinson, writing in the *Journal of Accountancy*, suggested that just as it is common practice on the part of corporations and individuals to retain (legal) counsel on the basis of a yearly consultation fee, this practice might be extended to the public accountant and, with many other matters of similar character, form the duties of a *consulting accountant*, a position on which he then elaborates.[7] This is the second noted use of the term "consulting accountant"—the first was related to the commission of Deloitte in 1864 (see Chapter 1).

Within this evolving service base the CPA auditor was benefiting from precedent and the influences of the U.K. profession, while at the same time adapting to a legally based service stature bestowed by state licensing. From the first year of the American Institute in 1887, when 26 members were enrolled, up to the years before the American entry into World War

---

[6]F.A. Cleveland, "The Scope of the Profession of Accountancy," *The Journal of Accountancy,* November 1905, p. 52.

[7]A. Lowes Dickinson, "Accounting Practice and Procedure," *The Journal of Accountancy,* December 1908, pp. 100–1.

I, when nearly 1300 members were enrolled, the young profession was occupied with its own development—and in defining its purposes (see Table 1, Introduction).

The issue of the role of the public accountant as auditor, advisor, and consultant was being joined. The discussions were about the scope of a public accountant's work, the *accountant's* relationships with clients and the meaning of the public *accountant's* role in the rapidly industrializing economy. These discussions evoked conflict and controversy then as now and foretold the concerns of today.

A MODEL FOR THE AMERICAN PROFESSION

Writing about the "present position" of the accountancy profession in the *Journal* in 1909, Joseph Sterrett, an early professional leader, observed:

> First, after the manner of the age [accountancy] might merge with other existing professions, or with parts thereof, to form a composite profession including, perhaps, certain classes of work now conducted by engineers and possibly absorbing certain kinds of work now carried on by the legal profession and taking up the burden of that somewhat shadowy individual, the business advisor.[8]

Yet he temporized by adding that "some would urge that its [accountancy's] largest usefulness will be attained by specialization. . . ." He then enumerated a number of possible industry specializations but warned that these are too narrow, and then argued that there are really only two phases of accounting work, each presenting some distinctive features:

> One is analytic as typified by the audit and the examination. The other is synthetic or constructive, instances of which are

[8]J.E. Sterrett, "The Present Position and Probable Development of Accountancy as a Profession," *The Journal of Accountancy,* February 1909, p. 268.

found in the construction and installation of cost and other systems of accounts.[9]

He concluded:

Accountancy, then, is not to be a thing of shreds and patches but will, if those in whose hands its fortunes are entrusted fulfill their part, expand along the lines upon which it is now operating, growing in dignity and power until it will stand shoulder to shoulder in the estimation of the public with those older professions whose courses have been a laborious evolution of years and centuries. *Accountancy will offer within itself a field for the exercise of widely differing talents and while the individual members will vary in their scope and methods of practice they will still be in the true sense of the term and will ever take pride in being called accountants.*[10] (Emphasis supplied.)

This surely represented the early manifestation of continuing efforts to provide diverse and challenging opportunities within a coherent framework of the profession of public accounting. Accountants then, as now, seemed to enjoy the comparison of their young profession to an older, established profession. The utility of being so compared served to inspire and remind them of their individual and collective aspirations to become a respected and learned profession. The discussions did not end with mere comparisons, however.

Writing for the *Journal* in 1912, Herbert G. Stockwell, a practitioner, suggested the broader field for certified public accountants was in reality:

An extremely large field of opportunity for the expert accountant . . . bounded only when we reach the legitimate realm of the lawyer on one side and the engineer on the other.

---

[9]Sterrett, "Position and Probable Development," p. 271.
[10]Sterrett, "Position and Probable Development," p. 273.

He concluded:

> I urge upon all accountants, and particularly the members of
> the Institute, to prepare themselves to occupy the field of
> expert advisers of the businessman who is today confronted
> with problems which the accountant should best be able to
> solve.[11]

By 1915, a *Journal* editorial by A.P. Richardson noted the
contrast between the emerging accounting professions in the
United Kingdom and the United States. He quoted a British
accountant: "Accountants in America seem to feel called upon
to give advice. No British accountant would dream of offering an opinion. His work is concerned with revealed facts
and not with any deductions therefrom."[12] This seems to
contradict inferences drawn from testimony in the House of
Lords discussed in Chapter 1, but it reflects a view of the
factual nature of early audits performed in the United Kingdom, which did not propose to give "advice."

Market forces, and the demand for expert services, drive
the direction of those services in accounting as in any en-
deavor. W.C. Heaton, writing in the *Journal* in 1925, stated:
"The fact is that the accountant cannot always limit com-
pletely the character of work he does. The circumstances lead
naturally toward and sometimes into fields of administration,
engineering and law."[13]

Speaking to the annual meeting of the Institute in 1920,
W.B. Gower noted:

> During the past three years the advisory functions of the
> public accountants have reached their highest stage as a result

[11]Herbert G. Stockwell, "The Broader Field for Certified Public Accountants," *The
Journal of Accountancy*, January 1912, pp. 23–24.
[12]A.P. Richardson, "Scope of Accountancy," *The Journal of Accountancy*, June 1915,
pp. 457–58.
[13]W.C. Heaton, "Development of Modern Practice," *The Journal of Accountancy*, August 1925, p. 108.

of huge taxes based upon profits, excess profits, and invested capital. These factors . . . are intimately related to and saturated with accounting concepts . . . that are almost unintelligible to laymen and difficult of comprehension even for lawyers.[14]

CONSULTING SERVICES: A FOCUS ON "PERMANENT RESPONSIBILITY"

Accountants outside of public practice also shared views about the role of the public accountant as described in the early issues of the *Journal*. In an address before the annual meeting of public accountants in 1914, Charles G. DuBois, comptroller of American Telephone and Telegraph, questioned whether public accountants should accept assignments outside established areas of practice (which he defined as auditing, systems consulting, and engagements relating to "business difficulties," such as reorganizations or changes in ownership of management). He pointed out that the work of the corporate accountant was better promoted in those instances where *permanent responsibility* and expertness as to the business were important to a project. He insisted:

I think the public accountant loses the respect of corporation managers for the work that he can do to advantage by soliciting work that, from the nature of the case, can only be developed and handled successfully by *permanent employees responsible for results*. If my view of the division of labor as between corporate accountants and the public accountants is economically sound, it will doubtless be recognized by public accountants that a part of attaining high professional standards sometimes consists of honestly recommending to their clients a course which means less employment for the public practitioner. Other professions, notably medicine and law,

[14]William B. Gower, "Advisory Accountancy," *The Journal of Accountancy*, October 1920, p. 268.

meet exactly this condition and accountancy cannot maintain a high professional status without solving such problems on the same plane.[15] (Emphasis added)

THE CHIEF CHARACTERISTIC OF THE ACCOUNTANT—INDEPENDENCE

A brochure written about 1895 by the original American-born partners of a Big Eight firm, Charles Waldo Haskins and Elijah Watt Sells, contains the following description of qualifications required of the public accountant.

> The qualifications of accountants engaged in making *independent* audits, in revising accounts, or investigating corporate affairs should be unquestioned integrity, appreciation of the gravity and confidential character of the responsibility . . . and strength of purpose, in order that the results of their work would be properly and fearlessly stated.[16] (Emphasis added)

In the midst of all the discussion over services to be offered, the business community had not only focused on the special expertise of the accountant, it had focused on another and more important difference—the accountant's impartial posture.

The value of this difference was confirmed in the view of managers who sought such services. A. DuPont Parker, who had risen to prominence as a Denver railroad and businessman, commented at the American Institute's annual meeting in 1909 that:

> When I interview an accountant today, I do not expect him to give me simply a balance sheet. I expect him to tell me

---

[15]Charles G. DuBois, "Accounting Conditions and Prospects," *The Journal of Accountancy*, October 1914, p. 251.

[16]E.A. Kracke, "Auditing Standards as Measures of the Auditor and His Procedures," *The Journal of Accountancy*, September 1946, p. 204.

certain things and define them. . . . And I will tell you why. . . . The reason I do this is because I stand before a man who has no axe to grind. . . . That is, I say, the *chief characteristic* of the accountant.[17] (Emphasis added)

Again, in 1908, Sells remarked that:

The position of the public accountant in respect to corporations and their management is always an independent one. Unlike the attorney he is not expected to make out a case. The character of the service he renders is impersonal.[18]

Taken together, historical research warrants suggesting that as early as 1900 a concept of independence was developing in the United States. Furthermore, statements such as the one by Reckitt, above, indicate that an awareness of public responsibility accompanied the concept.[19]

Professor R. Glen Berryman, reporting in 1974 on his research into the development of independence, states:

Independent status for the auditor appears to have emerged slowly as a major concern. . . . The American Institute . . . did not appear to have been actively concerned with independence until about 1930, although an amendment to the . . . organization bylaws in 1907 did recognize the desirability of avoiding incompatible or inconsistent occupations.[20]

Barbara D. Merino, however, points out that early American practitioners felt that independence could not be successfully

---

[17]A. DuPont Parker, "Accounting as a Steppingstone to Executive Work," *American Association of Public Accountants Yearbook*, 1909, p. 116.

[18]R. Glen Berryman, "Auditor Independence: Its Historical Development and Some Proposals for Research," *Contemporary Auditing Problems*, proceedings of the 1974 University of Kansas Symposium on Auditing Problems, ed. Howard F. Stettler, p. 2.

[19]Edward W. Younkins, "A History of Auditor's Independence in the U.S.," *The Accounting Historians Notebook*, Spring 1983, p. 1. (Author's note: It appears that Younkins has found another source of the quote used above by Barr.)

[20]Berryman, "Auditor Independence," p. 3.

reduced to rules, rather it had to be an *habitual state of mind*. To conclude that little was done because no written rules existed was to ignore the fact that important practitioners considered independence a *cultural ought*. To reduce the issue to a simple rule of conduct would be unwise. For rules they felt could not guarantee conduct; instead it would be essential to form a state of mind, a thought habit through appropriate education and carefully monitored experience of those entering the profession. They felt that to condemn all who participated in activities which were described as potentially compromising would be as foolhardy as concluding that those who simply followed the rules were, in fact, independent.[21] That this profound notion has persisted to the present time can be seen from the headnote to the AICPA's professional code of ethics: "A man should *be* upright; not be *kept* upright."[22]

Frederick Hurdman, writing in October 1931, demonstrated the difficulty of proscription and the delicate nature of independence:

> There can be no disputing the fact that in relations with clients the accountant should maintain his independence, and yet some of our best clients are those who depend upon us to a very large extent for guidance in the conduct of their business. It requires a very fine sense of balance at all times to preserve that independence and still maintain the closest of business and perhaps social relationships.[23]

[21]Barbara D. Merino, "The Professionalization of Accountancy in America: A Comparative Analysis of Selected Practitioners 1900–1925," Ph. D. dissertation, University of Alabama, 1975, pp. 228–29.
[22]American Institute of Certified Public Accountants, *AICPA Professional Standards* (vol. B): *Accounting and Review Services, Ethics, Bylaws, International Accounting, International Auditing, Management Advisory Services, Quality Control, Tax Practice*, sec. ET 51, Chicago: Commerce Clearing House, June 1, 1984, p. 4281.
[23]Frederick H. Hurdman, "Relation of Client and Accountant," *The Journal of Accountancy*, October 1931, p. 297.

One thing is certain, Hurdman noted:

> The accountant must be careful to guard against putting himself in a position where he has difficulty in applying an independent and unbiased judgment to any problem which may be presented to him for consideration. Therefore, generally speaking, an accountant should not accept appointment as a director or officer of a corporation whose books and accounts he audits unless the stock of that corporation be privately owned by a limited number of persons and the public generally is not affected thereby. . . .[24]

Hurdman also advised:

> Great care should be exercised that the auditor does not place himself in the position of having accepted a favor from management by being permitted to share in some benefit before a like offer is made to the public.

He concluded:

> It would appear that while no fixed rule can be laid down, the accountant should keep in mind the necessity at all times of preserving an independent relationship and so arranging his investments that he does not take advantage of the public nor permit any hoped for gain in market values to influence in any degree his impartial review and presentation of the facts.[25]

SCOPE OF SERVICES—EARLY VIEWS

The sphere of accountants' practice was, by 1925, being openly debated in the pages of the *Journal of Accountancy*. Richardson, the *Journal* editor, observed:

[24]Hurdman, "Client and Accountant," p. 297.
[25]Hurdman, "Client and Accountant," p. 304.

Accountancy is developing two schools of thought, . . . eccentric and concentric. The eccentric school is more aggressive and ready to spread out into fields new and untried and in short to do all things which may seem to be required by a client whether those things are of accountancy or otherwise. The concentric school has taken as its motto: "Sutor ne supre crepidam judicaret" . . . or "Let the cobbler stick to his last."[26]

An eminent member found on the conservative (i.e., "concentric") side was George O. May of Price Waterhouse, who wrote to the editor of the *Journal:*

It is an open question whether the present tendency to encourage the profession constantly to extend the scope of its activities is not fraught with more danger to it than the disesteem of those days. . . .[27]

Arthur Andersen, another pioneer of the profession and founder of the firm, held a more expansive view. He commented in an address to an Institute regional meeting in Chicago in November 1925:

In the experience of the past 10 years the businessman has found that advice from an accounting viewpoint may have high cash value in the form of taxes saved or refunded, war contracts liquidated, in recapitalizations and refinancings effected advantageously. . . . The present-day accountant who is alert will grasp every opportunity to foster this attitude by increasing the constructive value of all normal work and seeking newer and broader fields of service to business management. . . . In filling the function of advisor or consultant to management the accountant is thus entering fields of investigative work which mark a distinctive advance over the earlier

[26]A.P. Richardson, "The Accountant's True Sphere," *The Journal of Accountancy,* September 1925, pp. 190–91.
[27]George O. May, Letter, *The Journal of Accountancy,* September 1925, p. 191.

conceptions of the scope of his service and which deal with the broad aspects of business as a whole.[28]

He concluded by saying:

It is my profound conviction that the accountant of the future will prosper and consolidate his position in the business world in proportion to his breadth of vision and willingness to accept these responsibilities of larger service to industry.[29]

Other accountants, including J.O. McKinsey, who founded a major consulting firm bearing that name, also proposed to extend the duties of the public accountant. His suggestions that accountants be compensated on the basis of retainer where there is continuous service and on value of service and ability to pay rather than on per diem were viewed as radical by correspondents and authors who cited McKinsey's article as jeopardizing the audit role.[30] For "unless he draws the line," wrote Herbert Freeman in a following issue of the *Journal*, "and a very definite line, at that point, he runs the real danger of losing his status as a critic and thus failing properly to perform his function as an auditor. . . ." For while Freeman acknowledged it was fitting to consider "whether the accountant could serve the business community in two capacities," it would have to be considered that the accountant who enters into the *administration* of a business is disqualified as an auditor of that business."[31] He urged, instead, that accountants "look askance" at engagements which lead them into the executive field or those which charge them with the

---

[28]Arthur Andersen, "The Accountant's Function as Business Advisor," *The Journal of Accountancy*, January 1926, pp. 18–19.
[29]Andersen, "Accountant's Function," p. 21.
[30]J.O. McKinsey, "Modern Tendencies in Accounting Practice," *The Journal of Accountancy*, April 1925, p. 305.
[31]Herbert C. Freeman, "Some Thoughts on Modern Tendencies," *The Journal of Accountancy*, May 1925, p. 363.

responsibilities of administration until the status of the profession is established by legislative action. This view is consistent with the earlier charge to the public accountants by DuBois that they should avoid work better developed and handled successfully by, for example, *permanent employees* responsible for results.

Discussing the role of the public accounting profession in their 1928 edition of *Principles of Auditing*, Eric Kohler and Paul Pettengill provide the following view in a chapter entitled "Audits—Their Scope and Purpose." Audit engagements are listed as:

1. General audit.
2. The balance sheet audit.
3. The detailed audit.
4. The cash audit.
5. The cost of systems audit.
6. The continuous or periodic audit.
7. Special investigations.

The authors comment as well that:

> The accountant's duties are now manifold and he is called into consultation on matters involving all kinds of business problems. Generally, the *scope of services* an accountant may render includes the following:
>
> 1. Determination of the financial condition and earnings of a business for:
>   (a) officers, directors;
>   (b) partners or stockholders;
>   (c) bankers or investors. . . .
> 2. Investigations and reporting on such specific points as:
>   (a) A patent infringement;
>   (b) Federal income taxes;
>   (c) Embezzlement or fraud. . . .;
>   (d) Statements for "blue sky" commissions; [registrations statements at the state level]

(e)   General and cost accounting methods in use;
(f)   Bankruptcy and insolvency situations;
(g)   Reorganizations;
(h)   Partnership disputes;
(i)   Fire losses;
(j)   Budgets.

Kohler and Pettengill also speculated that:

> Lately there has been considerable agitation by the American
> Institute of Accountants urging public accountants to take
> advantage of the growing feeling on the part of businessmen
> and others that accountants are the most suitably qualified to
> fill the position of receiver. . . . Further, public accountants,
> as a rule, are unusually well qualified to act as arbitrators in
> commercial and trade disputes. . . .[32] (Emphasis supplied.)

In these latter areas, CPAs have not been successful in
establishing a position. Another prospective area of service,
that of CPAs serving as registrars of corporate securities, was
discussed, considered, and discouraged in a March 1928 editorial in the *Journal.* A California ruling had not recognized
a CPA's application to serve as a registrar. The editor commented with understatement that "it does not seem probable
that the opinion rendered by the commissioner of corporations in California will excite any violent opposition in the
minds of accountants generally."[33] All of this suggests that
not every field in which CPAs took an interest became a line
of service.

SCOPE OF SERVICES—EARLY EXAMPLES

The discussion and early debate over service scope, dedication to a mental state of independence, and visions of the

---

[32]Kohler and Pettengill, *Principles,* p. 16.
[33]A.P. Richardson, "Accountants Not Accepted as Registrars," *The Journal of Accountancy,* March 1928, p. 203.

future—eccentric or concentric—might, however, best be understood in light of what these early professionals did, and not just what they said. Some evidence as to engagements of the period and a general appreciation for the specific type of services rendered would be helpful to assess correspondence between what was practiced and what was preached during an era in which the audit service was determined by the market, not by law.

Advertising by public accountants prior to 1900 was commonly found in trade publications. In the October 26, 1880, issue of one such publication, advertisements are found by Selden R. Hopkins, Consulting and Expert Accountant; William B. Veysey, Professional Accountant; and others.[34] These two individuals would later attain prominence in the emerging CPA movement. One of Hopkins' specialties was to "render assistance to lawyers in the examination of accounts in litigation." In the 1980s, a century later, we refer to this as "litigation support services."

Haskins and Sells, two of the first CPAs in New York state, met when they were employed to assist the Dockery Commission in evaluating the "efficiency" of various agencies of the executive branch of the federal government in the 1890s.

Another principal form of service, mentioned early as "Audits for Management," was more commonly identified as "Investigations." In a pre-World War I edition of his auditing text, Robert H. Montgomery notes:

Part of the work of the professional auditor is designated, not as an audit, but as an investigation. There is here an actual distinction, just as the work of an accountant may be differentiated from that of an auditor. . . . Investigations are usually undertaken in connection with the sale of a business to a corporation or other purchaser for the purpose of obtaining special information relative to finances or general affairs or

[34]*The Book-Keeper,* October 26, 1880, p. 127.

with respect to alleged fraudulent transactions or into the profits derived from the manufacture of infringing articles, etc.[35]

Arthur Andersen's published firm history reports that it:

> Developed financial investigation reports which went into many phases of a business other than financial and accounting, including labor relations, availability of raw materials, plants, products, markets, effectiveness of the organization and future prospects. . . . The risks of this type of work were considerable but the results were helpful in establishing the reputation of the firm . . . for the reports were used by investment banking firms and others as a basis for financing enterprises. With the crash of 1929, financing engagements dwindled and this type of work . . . was practically discontinued in 1930 . . . however . . . some of the techniques developed in the financial investigation . . . were adopted in the firm's regular auditing procedures. . . .[36]

In 1908 the firm of Touche, Niven & Co. established a production cost department, managed by a cost expert. While the department was discontinued in 1911, the firm history notes that this event "foreshadowed the future and the growth in later years of management services. . . ."[37]

Other firms found that the effort of World War I had opened new areas of service as well. As noted by James Don Edwards, the "expansion of the audit function [into the management services field] had started during World War I when Arthur Young & Co. was asked to work for the British Gov-

[35]Robert Montgomery, *Auditing Theory and Practice*, New York: Ronald, 1912, p. 502.
[36]Arthur Andersen & Co., *The First Fifty Years: 1913–1963*, Chicago: Arthur Andersen & Co., 1963, p. 32.
[37]Touche Ross & Co., "Touche Ross: A Biography," *Tempo*, Special 25th Anniversary Issue, 1972.

ernment on a contract with Remington [Arms] Company."[38]

The growth of government at local and national levels—influenced by the efforts of national emergencies such as World War I, the impact of income taxation on corporations, the booming industrial economy founded on automobile manufacturing—created an expanded market demanding accountants' services. Accounting was to become the "middle class profession" creating career opportunities for individuals within CPA firms and as financial executives in industry. Within the public practice element, the principal focus of this study, firms developed specialties to address the needs of the marketplace.

The firm of Ernst & Ernst—whose letterhead suggested a special expertise in systems—issued in 1913 the "opinion" shown in Exhibit 1.

In 1903 Price Waterhouse made a decision to enter the field of municipal accounting. The firm received its first municipal engagement in the latter part of that year, a consultation for the City of Minneapolis to devise a modern and uniform system of accounts.[39] During this same period, Coopers & Lybrand (then Lybrand, Ross Bros. & Montgomery), provided services to auditors of a historical exhibition; to the treasurers of both major national political parties; and to the Canal Board of the State of New York to determine cost and expense factors on barge and terminal contracts. In 1921, Coopers was appointed by President Harding to arrange for the taking of a physical inventory and preparation of asset information for the Emergency Fleet Corp., which had spent several billion dollars during World War I but had no reliable

---

[38]James Don Edwards, *History of Public Accounting in the United States*, 1960, reprint, University, Alabama: The University of Alabama Press, 1978, p. 207.
[39]C.W. DeMond, *Price, Waterhouse & Co. in America*, New York: Price Waterhouse & Co., 1951, p. 71.

Exhibit 1

ERNST & ERNST

CERTIFIED PUBLIC ACCOUNTANTS (OHIO)

IMPARTIAL AUDITS—SYSTEMS

NEW YORK	CLEVELAND	CHICAGO
HANOVER BANK BLDG	SCHOFIELD BLDG	1ST NAT'L BK BLDG

NEW YORK

February 25, 1913

Gentlemen:

In accordance with your request we made an examination of the books of account and records of the .... MANUFACTURING   COMPANY, ... at December 31st, 1912, and submit herewith our report.

We were limited in our examination to a verification of the assets and liabilities at the close of the year, but we have included a statement of operations as shown by the books including such adjustments as we found in verifying the assets and liabilities.

All work on uncompleted contracts up to the close of the year had been billed as sales and all known liabilities were entered on the books according to written certificate received by us from your Mr. ....

A great improvement was found in the records of your company over the condition prevailing at the beginning of the year, care having been taken to keep the accounts in balance and to enter on the books promptly all transactions affecting the financial condition or operations of the company.

WE HEREBY CERTIFY that we examined the books of account and records as above stated and in our opinion, based upon our examination and information submitted to us, the annexed Balance Sheet shows the true financial condition of the company at December 31st, 1912.

Very truly yours,

ERNST AND ERNST

Certified Public Accountants.

[Seal]

Source: Copy of original letter in author's file.

knowledge of where or how it had spent funds or what assets remained. The chairperson of the shipping board had declared it to be "the worst accounting mess in history."[40]

Haskins & Sells undertook a unique attest engagement in 1923, related to the publication of data included in a study. The firm issued a statement "certifying" as to the particulars of that report (Exhibit 2), as follows:

Exhibit 2 An Example of a Special Attest Report

Statement by
Haskins & Sells
Certified Public Accountants

Pursuant to engagement, we have reviewed the manuscript of your book *Analysis of the Interchurch Report on the Steel Strike* for the purpose of verifying, by comparison with their stated sources, the citations, quotations, statistics, and figures contained therein; and

WE HEREBY CERTIFY:

That all citations are accurate;

That all quotations, including excerpts in which the sequence of original passages has for clearness or brevity been varied, are accurate as to text and, in our opinion, fairly represent the meaning of their original context;

That all statistics and figures quoted have been verified by comparison with documents from which quoted and those subject to mathematical proof have been so proved; and

That all statistics are presented and used in accordance with generally accepted statistical practices.

(Signed) HASKINS & SELLS.

Source: Marshall Olds, *Analysis of the Interchurch World Movement Report on the Steel Strike,* New York: Putnam, 1922 (Arno Reprint, 1972).

[40]Lybrand, Ross Bros. & Montgomery, *Fiftieth Anniversary: 1898–1948,* New York: Lybrand, Ross Bros. & Montgomery, pp. 73–75.

Paul Grady, one of the leading accountants of his era, describes the special insolvency oversight engagement which Arthur Andersen & Co. undertook in 1932 to assist creditor banks on the collapse of the Insull utility empire. Loans had been advanced to Insull to build his pyramid of companies and to fund expansion:

> The banks suggested that the firm countersign checks. We did not want that kind of responsibility so I developed a voucher control procedure which would leave in tact all normal approval procedures by company employees and officials and superimpose our approval of vouchers before checks could be issued. . . . The unusual variety of work performed in the Insull situation by Arthur Andersen & Co. may raise a question or propriety in the minds of present-day readers. My analysis then and now [c. 1977] is that the services were entirely proper. . . . In my view, a monitoring approach which leaves in tact all of the companies' systems of authorization and approval, has nothing to do with the distributions or allocations in the accounts, has no power to originate transactions but merely to bring information on questionable disbursements before a panel of creditors for possible veto under an arrangement agreed to by debtor companies, is perfectly ₚroper as a public accounting engagement. Certainly the firm's independence was in no way impaired, nor were there any conflicts of interest. Arthur Andersen's membership on the panel was an agency relationship with the New York banks and was fully agreed to by all the Insull companies. He [Mr. Andersen] did not participate in any way with the monitoring work after the basic plan of operation had been approved.[41]

SUMMARY

The era of free markets for CPA services, which is characterized as the period before SEC-mandated audits, suggests

[41]Paul Grady, *Written Contributions of Selected Accounting Practitioners*, vol. 2, ed. V.K. Zimmerman, Urbana, IL: Center for International Education and Research in Accounting, 1978, pp. 17–19.

that expected economic behavior for "eccentric" action (expansion of practice) was counterd by those who were more conservatively oriented (concentric) and wished even to have the profession "confirmed in legislation" before taking on added practices. The dichotomy between proactive and reactive groups was clearly evident.

Many of the concerns over auditor independence known today appear in discussions and essays of this early period. Robert Montgomery expressed a synoptic view: "Our most precious asset is our independence in thought and action. Our method of expressing the use of our asset is by means of opinion or judgment."[42]

Some of the life cycles of CPA services originated and grew (shareholder audits) or developed only minimally (bankruptcy) during this period, and some services were proposed which never developed (arbitration and receivership). CPAs began to express desires to professionalize their discipline as practitioners in medicine and law had done.

Some assert that the "manifest destiny" of the CPA profession rests within those service areas not already claimed by established, legitimate professions, such as law and engineering. The first clear call for a separate consulting role is also found in the article by J.O. McKinsey—a role criticized by some, but ultimately developed by McKinsey and those like him into today's management consulting firms.

Independence as a concept was held by many to be a cultural ought, not a notion limited by sets of rules.

[42]Robert H. Montgomery, "Accountants' Limitations," *The Journal of Accountancy,* October, 1927, pp. 245–49.

3

Developing CPA Practice in The United States

THE EARLY SEC PERIOD—1933 TO 1946

It is not really independence, which some glib and uninformed writers discuss so freely, it is rather integrity, which is so necessary to the practice of a profession.[1]

Maurice E. Peloubet, 1944

[1]Maurice E. Peloubet, "Independence—A Blessed Word," *The Journal of Accountancy,* January 1944, p. 69.

With the passage of the Securities Acts in 1933 and 1934, Congress mandated an audit service but placed the function in the private sector. It has been debated whether the legislators focused clearly on a single concept of auditor independence in the legislative hearings which produced the acts. Perhaps they did not. Nevertheless, the profession's history for several decades can be told in part by tracing the process by which that concept would be shaped and the meaning it would acquire. As the absolute numbers of independent auditors increased dramatically in response to the demand for mandated audits and other services, so the posture of the auditor was defined to protect the integrity of the assurances the auditor provided regarding the financial statements of public companies.

It was also this period which saw the "institutional commitment" to what today are called management consulting services by public accountants. Such services were deeply rooted in the history of the profession, and had become regarded as typical activities, both in the United States and in the United Kingdom. Now the requirements of global war were to evoke the consulting role of CPAs as a vital, permanent, *strategic knowledge resource*.

What would need to be reconciled was the relationship of *independent* auditing with the strategic market demand for consulting services. For the United States was initiating a historic effort to gain and maintain a dominant role in world affairs militarily, and then economically and politically.

A PROFILE OF THE CPA PROFESSION

Describing CPAs on the eve of the eventful period leading to New Deal legislation and the establishment of the SEC, *Fortune* magazine wrote in June 1932:

> Towards the turn of the century there sprang up in this country a new profession. Already established abroad, it followed

English investments to the U.S., watched over them, took root. Today it is no overstatement to say that there are preeminently three professions upon whose ethics as well as upon whose skills modern society depends: law, medicine, and certified public accounting.[2]

During the period from 1933 through the immediate years following World War II, the public accounting profession again experienced tremendous growth. Two CPA organizations, The American Institute of Accountants and The American Society of Certified Public Accountants, rival associations representing the U.S. profession on the eve of the passage of the securities laws, had altogether a membership of over 4000 CPAs. The two organizations merged after the passage of the securities laws. Some have inferred that this division and the subsequent reconciliation of the groups were important institutional factors both before and after legislation—before in the sense that the divisiveness detracted from the solidarity of the profession, and after in that the reconciliation indicated the awareness of the benefits of a united professional organization.

There had been a total membership slightly larger than 1000 at the turn of the century. Immediately following World War II, before the full force of another wave of expansion had yet to be felt, the American Institute, which then represented the merged national membership, would grow to a total of 11,000 members (see Table 1, Introduction). This nucleus group offered services of substantial depth and breadth to a national, and often global, marketplace. At the same time it was working within its own ranks to form the basis of accounting and auditing standards, and the procedures of self-regulation expected of a profession.

Within this context and demographic limitations, one can begin to assess the scope of consulting services and independence issues—with perhaps one added point of considera-

[2]"Certified Public Accountants," *Fortune*, June 1932, p. 63.

tion. The education and experience requirements of the CPA profession were still principally based on a minimum of a high school education and several years of working for a CPA to obtain "qualifying" experience. Many staff persons held only seasonal positions in CPA firms, and total partnership in the so-called leading firms was, even in grand total, only a fraction of what was reached by the mid-1980s.

INDEPENDENCE AND THE SECURITIES ACTS

Securities legislation created a potentially lucrative service franchise for the "independent public accountant." Schedule A of the Securities Act of 1933 requires that balance sheets and profit and loss statements be certified by an *independent* public or certified public accountant. Similarly, Section 12 of the Securities Exchange Act of 1934 gives the SEC the authority to require that applications for the registration of a security contain financial statements which have been "certified . . . by independent public accountants." And the 1934 Act also authorizes the Commission to specify that annual reports filed with the SEC contain financial statements which have been "certified . . . by *independent* public accountants."[3] Both laws also created for public accountants an enormous potential liability *and* a possibly hostile market—the latter since corporations were now required to use the services of an auditor in compliance with federal law. The "compliance audit" stood in contrast to "voluntary" shareholder audits which were encouraged by Dickinson in 1902, and under-

---

[3]U.S. Securities and Exchange Commission, *Codification of Financial Reporting Policies of the Securities and Exchange Commission,* Section 601, April 15, 1982.

Regulation S-X of the SEC reads: *The Commission will not recognize any person as a certified public accountant who is not duly registered and in good standing as such under the laws of the place of his residence or principal office. The commission will not recognize any person as a public accountant who is not in good standing and entitled to practice as such under the laws of the place of his residence or principal office.*

taken by a large number of public corporations before the market catastrophe of the late 1920s. Compliance auditing also provided incentive for auditors to "sell" their certificates since the market for the service was seemingly vast and requirements for auditing and reporting were as yet unestablished.

CONGRESS AND AUDITOR INDEPENDENCE

What was Congress's intent? One researcher reports that the independence of auditors was not focused on at the 1933 Senate hearings. Further, he notes that while the Securities Acts were carefully conceived and debated, the duties of the auditors were not of great interest to the members of Congress and that "an analysis of the legislative history indicates a lack of knowledge about auditing on the part of congressmen and less than a vigorous interest in the topic when it was raised at hearings."[4]

Another historian, Professor Committe, asserts that a clear conception of independence, used in conjunction with the role of public accountants as auditors, indeed emerged from the congressional hearings of 1933 and 1934. He implies that research into the content of government documents supports the position that "a public accountant-auditor is independent only if he or she acts only on the public investor's behalf as an advocate of the public interest and has no association or relationship with the auditee organization such that the interests of the auditee organization could influence the audit judgment making of the auditor."[5]

[4]Jeremy Wiesen, *The Securities Acts and Independent Auditors: What Did Congress Intend?*, Commission on Auditors' Responsibilities, Research Study No. 2, New York: AICPA, 1978, pp. 8–9.
[5]Bruce Edward Committe, "Structuring a Public Accounting Audit Independence Theory from a Document Study of U.S. Congressional Testimony," Ph. D. dissertation, University of Alabama, 1983.

In describing the result of the hearings, SEC Accounting Series Release (ASR) No. 81 states that:

> The committee considered at length the value to investors and to the public of an audit by accountants *not connected* with the company or management and whether the additional expense to industry of an audit by independent accountants was justified by the expected benefits to the public. The committee also considered the advisability and feasibility of requiring the audit to be made by accountants on the staff of the agency administering the Act.[6] (Emphasis added.)

Given the variety of views resulting from research in the area, the customary roles which have emerged since these hearings over a half century ago, and the apparent disagreement among scholars, it seems prudent to consider the ways in which independence was observed. The "cultural ought" approach—based on personal principles, as described in Chapter 2, was to be overshadowed by rules and codes of conduct. The SEC ASRs on independence and the AICPA Rules of Professional Conduct would parallel and *contrast* one another over the next three decades, setting forth a basis deemed appropriate for behavior.

In the view of some, this rule-oriented approach would provide a better understanding of the meaning of the term "independence." For it was this *acquired meaning* of independence which was made to matter most and which became the *essence* of the debate.

The expected social guarantee of independence took on increased importance to safeguard the public against improper behavior by professional corporate managers which would not accord with the best interest of investors and shareholders. The shock of the "crash" of the stock markets and public concern over abuses based on speculation related to industrial expansion in the 1920s had brought an end to one

---

[6]U.S. Securities and Exchange Commission, "Independence of Certifying Accountants," ASR No. 81 (December 11, 1958), in *Accounting Series Releases and Staff Accounting Bulletins,* Chicago: Commerce Clearing House, June 1, 1981, p. 3150.

era. Intellectuals such as Professor Ripley of Harvard and Professors Berle and Means of Columbia found political support for establishing a federal regulatory presence in capital markets. The agent for fulfilling the responsibilities envisioned in these views was to be the CPA as public auditor. The question remained however: "Whose agent was the CPA?"

Business might view the CPA as a government operative—an added cost imposed by compliance legislation. The public might view the CPA as a public agent entrusted with public well being. Government officials might view the CPA as an extension of the SEC, providing on-site review of public corporations which, due to government's limited resources, often had to be delegated. The CPA had to construct a self-image and an identity consistent with these several and conflicting expectations. Everyone, including the profession, would find that the process of shaping this role—that of a competent and independent auditor—would require both time and compromise.

And agreement on the results of the process could not always be expected. An offended or neglected party could seek the support of the courts, the SEC, legislators, and self-regulatory boards within the CPA profession.

Years, even decades, would pass before the issues would be properly balanced. Chief among them were technical competence and professional independence. No sooner was an equilibrium achieved than a new service opportunity or market expectation arose and the process would begin anew—too often without a knowledge of tradition and without the benefit of an "institutional memory," in which the young CPA profession had not fully seen a need to invest.

MANDATES FOR INDEPENDENCE—PROFESSIONAL AND GOVERNMENTAL

The simple, yet profound, effect of Congress's decision to involve independent accountants in the process of registration and reports filed with the SEC was to place the CPA

profession in the position of having to act on its own authority
to establish independence guidelines for *all* CPAs, not just
those involved in filings of publicly held companies, lest the
rules set forth by the SEC in independence become *de facto*
the rules of the profession. Therein lay a difficult political
effort. Many CPA practitioners, who stood to lose directorships or voting share interests in promising ventures because
they also provided audit services to closely held companies,
would be tempted to resist any diminishment of their personal fortune just to assist larger firms who in their audits of
SEC companies were constrained to limit their involvement.

To the extent that the CPA profession could move ahead
in establishing the *concept* of independence, any rules limiting
the factual and economic relationships of CPAs working with
nonpublic clients could be more readily promoted with the
view toward maintaining a "single" unified CPA profession
instead of a "two-tiered profession." (Those engaged in public-company audit work versus everyone else.) Frederick H.
Hurdman noted this when writing in 1942:

> Until some years ago, certified public accountants considered
> themselves, perhaps correctly, as a professional group in whose
> affairs the public took little interest. Recently, however, the
> profession has been somewhat surprised to find how serious
> an interest the public has developed in accounting and au-
> diting. It may be safely assumed that banks, other credit gran-
> tors and stock exchanges and other public bodies will hold
> certified public accountants responsible for the observance of
> standards just as high as those enforced by the SEC.[7]

In the process of attempting to shift the real practice of
the CPA profession toward the ideal of independence, both
the SEC and the Institute would find ample opportunity to
express differing views and take opposing positions.[8]

---

[7]Frederick H. Hurdman, "Independence of Auditors," *The Journal of Accountancy,*
January 1942, p. 60.
[8]Michael Firth, "Perceptions of Auditor Independence and Official Ethical Guidelines," *The Accounting Review,* July 1980.

However, not until the impact of World War II on the scope of services became evident—dramatically amplifying the ability of CPAs to provide vital services, much as a national resource—did the full potential for the CPA as both auditor and consultant become apparent. So dominant was the preoccupation with perfecting the process of auditing that the profession did not foresee clearly the inadequacy of constraining independence via narrow, objective rules—instead of maintaining a personal-cultural view above the mere level of rules.

Since the market for the audit seemed to have limitless growth potential, a strategic shift toward independence "rules" seemed an appropriate long-term solution to achieving the difficult equilibrium expected by the various parties related to securities legislation. Altogether, this period of development of the CPA profession was audit-centered—almost entirely identified with the performance of audit work. Students preparing for the profession were directed toward accounting and auditing subjects.

An important aspect of this period was the give-and-take which the profession and the SEC utilized to develop the concept of independence. First emphasis was placed on general limits. From the SEC's view, there could be "no financial interest" held by the auditor. Next came case-by-case examples, as in ASR No. 22 (1941); and therein came an interpretation of what was *considered* or what *appeared* to be independent or not independent—as differentiated from what was *in fact* a lack of independence. Rules would be drafted by the SEC and the Institute in an attempt to address the issues identified during each of these stages. By 1947 the CPA Institute would adopt a formulation of general auditing standards which could be likened to a decalogue or creed for auditors. The major precept of this decalogue was that of independence.[9]

Practitioners felt strongly that the auditing standards, which

[9]E.A. Kracke, "Auditing Standards as Measures of the Auditor and His Procedures," *The Journal of Accountancy,* September 1946, p. 207.

have endured to the present time, captured the essence of proper professional behavior. Paul Grady stated:

> The "oath" of the accounting profession is embodied in the ten generally accepted auditing standards approved and adopted by the membership of the American Institute of Certified Public Accountants. Each of the standards is stated in clear and unequivocal language. While they may be explained and discussed at great length, individually and in relationship to each other, any competent CPA who is dedicated to the task of fulfilling the public trust of independent auditing will understand and abide by the philosophy inherent in the standards.[10]

EPISODES IN SEC AND AICPA ATTEMPTS TO DEVELOP INDEPENDENCE

The Federal Trade Commission, which administered the securities laws until the SEC was formed, issued an early regulation under the 1933 Act which provided that an accountant would not be considered independent with respect to any person (registrant) in whom the accountant had any interest, directly or indirectly, or with whom the accountant was connected as an officer, agent, employee, promoter, underwriter, trustee, partner, director, or person performing a similar function.

Subsequently, when the SEC undertook administration of the securities laws it was persuaded to amend the independence regulations to prohibit relationships which were deemed *substantial* in either a direct or indirect fashion. In 1937 the SEC held, in ASR No. 2, that an accountant cannot be deemed independent if he or she is or has been during the period under review an officer or director of the registrant or if he

---

[10]Paul Grady, *Written Contributions of Selected Accounting Practitioners*, vol. 2, ed., V.K. Zimmerman, Urbana, IL: Center for International Education and Research in Accounting, 1978, p. 473.

or she holds an interest in the registrant that is significant with respect to its capital or the accountant's own personal fortune. The limit was one percent of an accountant's personal fortune; anything larger would be questioned by the SEC. Later, however, the term "substantial" was again dropped by the SEC.

According to John Carey, the issue of appearance of independence could be traced to this very first enactment of the SEC rule, which provided that an accountant would not be *considered* independent by the Commission if he or she were an officer or director of the client, or if he or she had a substantial financial interest in the enterprise. A resolution of similar import had been approved at the Institute's 1934 annual meeting, but an ethical rule imposing such a restriction had been rejected by the Council of the Institute when it had been proposed. Later, that rule would be adopted, in 1941, with the proviso that the financial interest be "substantial"; these ideas would ultimately form the basis of Ethical Rule 13 as approved in 1950. The key word in the SEC rule was *considered,* and as Carey states, "the element of appearance, in addition to the element of actuality, was officially introduced into the concept of independence as it applied to the accounting profession."[11]

INDEPENDENCE IN FACT

An editorial in the April 1940 *Journal* asked the "ultimate" independence question: "Can a certified public accountant be wholly independent of the client who pays his fee and controls the tenure of his appointment?" The editor suggested that the issue could be reduced to even more specific terms, namely: "Will the accountant permit a client to influence him to express the opinion that the financial statements

[11]John L. Carey, *The Rise of the Accounting Profession to Responsibility and Authority: 1937–1969,* vol. 2, New York: AICPA, 1970, p. 177.

fairly present the facts when the accountant doesn't believe that they really do so?" Responding to his own question, the editor noted: "The heavy direct personal liability which a professional accountant assumes would be an effective deterrent to sacrifice of independence even if consideration of ethics and honor were overcome by temptation."[12]

Several years later, in 1945, the editor reopened the issue in response to a critic who had remarked that "no profession ancillary to business no matter how high-minded . . . can really be independent."[13] The editor responded that:

> The accountant in every auditing engagement has a co-employer, the public. If his work is not satisfactory to those who ultimately make use of it he will no longer be useful to the client who pays his fee. It is therefore . . . not necessarily nobility or extraordinary strength of character which makes the accountant independent but primarily an instinct of *professional self-preservation*.[14] (Emphasis supplied.)

The editor then concluded:

> There is nothing wonderful about his independence, and only those hesitate to recognize it whose knowledge or experience does not enable them to understand its source.[15]

Here then is one of the first public references, ignoble as it sounds, to enlightened self-interest as the ultimate guarantor of independence. Bereft of all the trappings of high purpose and reduced to its sheerest economic appeal, it represents one of the strongest incentives for professional CPAs to *preserve* their independence in the face of avarice.

---

[12]John L. Carey, "Independence of Auditors," *The Journal of Accountancy*, April 1940, p. 250.
[13]John L. Carey, ed., "Independence of Accountants," *The Journal of Accountancy*, February 1945, p. 92.
[14]Carey, ed., "Independence of Accountants," p. 93.
[15]*Ibid.*

INDEPENDENCE IN APPEARANCE

As the reality of this enlightened self-interest argument was being identified, the other element of independence—a much subtler, more difficult element—gained attention. When it was fully expressed, it would become the issue of independence in appearance.

In ASR No. 22, the SEC had prepared a summary of findings on several independence cases. Hurdman, in analyzing the significance of this release, points out the "new" element of Commission concern:

> The Commission has rejected the theory that lack of independence can only be established by falsification of financial statements. The SEC has instead decided that to adopt such an interpretation would be to ignore the fact that one of the purposes of requiring a certificate by an independent accountant is to remove the possibility of impalpable and unprovable biases which an accountant may unconsciously acquire because of intimate nonprofessional contacts with his client. The requirement for certification by an independent public accountant is as much a guarantee against conscious falsification or intentional deception as it is a measure to ensure complete objectivity. It is in part to protect the accounting profession from the implications that slight carelessness or choice of a debatable accounting procedure is the result of bias or lack of independence that this Commission has in its prior decisions adopted objective standards. Viewing our requirements in this light, any inferences of a personal nature that may be directed against specific members of the accounting profession depend on the facts of a particular case and do not flow from the undifferentiated application of uniform objective standards.[16]

Within this release are the seeds of the issues related to unconscious and nonprofessional activities which could serve as

[16]Hurdman, "Independence of Auditors," p. 58.

a bias. If this standard were literally followed, it might be necessary for the auditor to adopt such an adversarial relationship vis-à-vis a client that any pleasant and constructive relationships might be viewed with suspicion. Such an idea, as we have seen, is not new, for traces of it were found in the testimony cited in Chapter 1 before the House of Lords. At that time it was recognized that not much more than a technical or compliance audit would be accomplished if such relationships were proscribed. The issue is: Can a constructive audit be established in an environment which has a premise of an adversarial relationship and suggests the lack of mutual respect and trust?

ASR No. 22 caused Hurdman to remark that "Any circumstances which might be held likely to induce such bias in the mind of the accountant may be held to be evidence of lack of independence." He concluded that the CPA "invites public criticism which may result in . . . professional disaster (when) he permits circumstances to arise which cast doubt on his independence, even though he may be sure that his state of mind is as independent as it could be." Hurdman was concerned that the "appearance of impropriety is only slightly less dangerous than the impropriety itself."[17] This view, while formed from early episodes including one where an individual CPA proposed to serve as both accountant and auditor, became generalized by some to constitute a "pristine" rationale for the *appearance* of independence.

The Institute's view on the matter was found in a *Journal* editorial (March 1944):

> Here are two approaches to the problem of independence. One is the application of what have been called objective standards, that is, rules describing certain relationships which the accountant must avoid or be found lacking in independence . . . . The other approach originates in the recognition

---

[17]Hurdman, "Independence of Auditors," p. 60.

that independence is an attitude of mind and a manifestation of integrity and character.

Those who hold this view maintain that independence should be challenged only with specific cause, such as lack of full disclosure or willful or careless misstatement, but not merely because an accountant has rendered a client various professional services generally recognized as entirely proper, while serving also as an independent auditor.

In clarifying the position of the professional certified public accountant, proper weight should be given to both points of view. Character, integrity, and enlightened self-interest are the fundamental bases of independence.

It would be unfair to impute subconscious bias as ground for finding an accountant to be lacking independence when no reasonable objective standard has been violated and there is no evidence of an error of omission or commission. The accountant should not be put into the position of being judged on the unprovable working of his mind. If an auditor were to avoid all relationships which might conceivably induce a bias in his subconscious mind, he would have to work in a social vacuum.[18]

One might also ask whether to deny any citizen the right to freedom of subconscious action would not seem to deny a basic human and constitutional right.

While the Institute was forming a response to the matter of bias as expressed in the language of ASR No. 22, the Commission was adopting Rule 2.01(c) of Regulation S-X relating to independence. SEC Chairman Ganson Purcell, writing for the *Journal of Accountancy*, noted that:

The Commission felt that we should express in the form of a rule our conviction of long standing that in considering whether an accountant was independent it was necessary to

---

[18]John L. Carey, ed., "SEC Release on Independence of Public Accountants," *The Journal of Accountancy*, March 1944, p. 180.

explore fully all the facts and circumstances of a particular
case. . . . We merely sought to outline in a more specific rule
what we had always felt in practice—that independence was
a question of fact, to be determined after examining all the
evidence that might bear upon the existence or non-existence
of that fact.[19]

The SEC seemed to have relented from the strictness of ASR
No. 22. There was some consolation in this statement that
independence in fact was still the issue. But the core of another facet of independence had now been identified in the
text of ASR No. 22—the idea of independence being influenced by activities other than those which could be objectively
identified and constrained. From the seeds of this idea would
emerge concerns over lack of independence in appearance
and attendant concerns over how a relationship between auditor and client could be influenced when other services were
being provided.

DEVELOPMENTS IN SCOPE OF CONSULTING SERVICES

As the economy struggled to recover from the national emergency of the Great Depression, another national crisis was
forming. Its swift political impact was to cause attention to
shift from concern about reforming the marketplace and the
economic system considered at fault at the time of the Depression to adapting that system to support the strategic effort
of a global war.

At the outbreak of World War II in England, scientists
were called to the assistance of the Air Force to attack the
critical problem of coordinating the newly developing early
warning radar systems with Air Force operations. This, in
turn, led to efficiency investigations related to communications and other systematic analyses—called "operations re-

[19]Ganson Purcell, "Cooperation between SEC and Public Accountants," *The Journal
of Accountancy*, August 1943, p. 155–156.

search." After the war, operations research techniques, alternatively called "management science," became even more widely used in industries beyond those principally involved in defense. These new techniques were incorporated into accounting advisory services, and the field of management advice and assistance became a steadily increasing proportion of the total volume of public accounting services.[20]

Furthermore, as businesspeople saw the potential for increased efficiency and cost savings from the applications of such techniques in planning and operations, they began to expect more from their internal and external accountants in the form of statistical and accounting reports. Accountants in firms such as Arthur Andersen & Co. began to plan for developing competence in these new areas and established operating divisions to provide them. The impact was foreseen, prophetically, by Donald Perry, writing in the *Accounting Review* in April 1944:

> Prior to the war the average accounting practice was largely composed of audit work and preparation of tax returns sweetened on occasion by nonrecurring system engagements or cases dealing with new financing. The scope of services rendered by accountants has been considerably extended in wartime, and it seems probable that the success of the profession in handling these varied assignments may result in a wider field of practice in the future.[21]

Perry's speculation was confirmed in the same periodical two years later by John Queenan, later to become managing partner of Haskins & Sells. Queenan noted:

> Accompanying the complex problems arising from the war, many of which have had a direct bearing on accounting, there has been an increasing tendency for business executives to

[20]John L. Carey, *The Rise of the Accounting Profession to Responsibility and Authority: 1937–1969*, vol. 2, p. 55.
[21]Donald P. Perry, "Professional Accounting Practice Today and Tomorrow," *The Accounting Review*, April 1944, p. 167.

seek the advice of the public accountant before the execution of a transaction. . . . In the exercise of his expanded functions he has become no less independent. As a matter of fact, his advice has been sought because of his independent thought as well as his wide accounting and business experience. There appears to be little doubt that this phase of his work will continue and develop in the future, since it offers business executives a valuable independent opinion as to the wisdom and propriety of proposed financial and business plans.[22]

Another emerging leader of the CPA profession during this period, Paul Grady, commented on the issue of the developing role of accounting as "an indispensable tool of business and government." He pointed out that the independent accountant through his wide accounting experience should be in a position to render valuable advisory or consulting service to his client, particularly on financial matters. He noted:

In addition to these broad constructive and creative services the independent accountant must discharge his full responsibilities as an independent auditor of financial statements, to all who may be entitled to rely on the statements. Our responsibility, insofar as the integrity of our work is concerned, is not a matter of "allegiance to business clients" but extends to society as a whole.[23]

THE CONSTANT PRESSURE OF CHANGE

From these observations and with the benefit of historical hindsight, it becomes clear that whatever the CPA profession was to become under the boon of SEC audit franchise, it was also to be transformed in the wake of the phenomenal changes of the American economy as it entered the postwar expansion

[22]John W. Queenan, "The Public Accountant of Today and Tomorrow," *The Accounting Review,* July 1946, p. 258.
[23]Grady, "Selected Accounting Practitioners," p. 65.

and addressed the challenges of international development. No one would foresee, however, that the CPA profession, then numbering only 12,000 Institute members, would now enter a period of explosive growth which would find American Institute memberships growing to 25,000 members by the mid-1950s and to nearly 50,000 members in the early 1960s (see Table 1, Introduction). The challenge to remain competent, in part addressed by an enhanced education requirement, was recognized. Henceforth, candidates for the CPA examination would possess a bachelor's degree with a concentration in business and accounting subjects.

As to independence, the issue was far from resolved, and yet the adoption of generally accepted auditing standards by the Institute in fact accorded full recognition of the auditor's responsibility for maintaining independence in fact. The issue of appearance, however, would now become the central concern.

Some, including academics such as A.C. Littleton and Bishop C. Hunt, engaged in printed debate over the matter of how best to afford the CPA an opportunity to achieve the appropriate level of independence. The issue they debated suggested that there was a relationship between an auditor's diligence and an auditor's independence. But Hunt felt that independence was consistently achieved within the context of audit diligence as outlined by Lord Justice Lopes in the Kingston Cotton Mill case:

> It is the duty of an auditor to bring to bear on the work he has to perform that skill, care and caution which a reasonably competent, careful and cautious auditor would use. What is reasonable care, skill and caution must depend upon the particular circumstances of each case. An auditor is not bound to be a detective . . . to approach his work with suspicion or with a foregone conclusion that something is wrong. He is a watch dog, but not a blood hound.[24]

---

[24]Bishop C. Hunt, "Auditor Independence," *The Journal of Accountancy*, June 1935, p. 456.

SUMMARY

Historians note that the early SEC period provided government and the young CPA profession substantial opportunities to improve the public trust in the capital markets by means of the legislated independent audit. However, critics of SEC action during the period are quick to suggest that the full potential of the period was not realized and that in many ways the SEC abandoned its legislative role in favor of private sector initiatives.[25] In the matter of independence, however, it is clear that constant pressure through rules and the emerging distinction between forms of independence would not be "glossed over" by the SEC. For in ASR No. 47 (1944), the SEC's chief accountant, William Werntz, reiterated the view of judging appearances:

> Certain relationships between an accountant and his client appear so apt to prevent the accountant from reviewing the financial statements and accounting procedures of a registrant with complete objectivity that the Commission has taken the position that existence of these relationships will preclude its finding that an accountant is, in fact, independent.[26]

These situations involved ownership, directorship, and family relationship cases. This view abetted the arguments which would later be put forth that certain forms of consulting services were "inherently" compromising in appearance and should be judged apt to impugn independence.

In these early attempts to identify issues and practices bearing upon independence, there are several examples and valuable lessons. But hindsight, aided by the hopeful gropings

[25]Robert Chatov, *Corporate Financial Reporting*, New York: Free Press, 1975.
[26]U.S. Securities and Exchange Commission, "Independence of Certifying Accountants," ASR No. 47 (January 25, 1944), in *Accounting Series Releases and Staff Accounting Bulletins*, Chicago: Commerce Clearing House, June 1, 1981, p. 3058.

of individuals of goodwill and experience, often were all that existed to guide the process. Many of the views expressed indicated that both philosophically and professionally different *meanings* were being ascribed to the term independence. Could it be that the meaning of independence was a function of the type of service the CPA performed? Decades later John Carey would remark that, "We can say with confidence that *audit* independence means integrity and objectivity."[27] (Emphasis supplied.) These were necessary elements, but are they sufficient?

[27]John L. Carey, "The Independence Concept Revisited," *The Ohio CPA Journal,* Spring, 1985, p. 6.

4

The CPA as Auditor

1947 TO 1961

Self-discipline by the profession will add immeasurably more to the stature and growth of the profession than rules applied to it by others.[1]

Richard S. Claire, 1943

[1]Richard S. Claire, "Accountants and Other Laymen," *The Arthur Andersen Chronicle*, December 1, 1943, p. 71.

POSTWAR DEVELOPMENTS

The different technical definitions of "independence" began to be reconciled during the period from 1947 to 1961, as both the SEC and the profession began to understand the full implications of a rapidly maturing audit function. To appear independent should the auditor hold *no* economic interest in a client or no *substantial* interest? This was resolved in favor of the former. Further attention was devoted to the dichotomy between independence *in fact* and independence *in appearance;* considerable lip service was given to the former as the latter became perceived as even more intricate amidst more promulgated and detailed rules of behavior. Also, renewed attention was being paid by professionals to independence as a fundamental characteristic that should apply to all of a CPA's services, be they auditing or consulting.

For along with attention to the audit function, the accounting professional also was giving increased attention to new and traditional consulting services. The AICPA was starting to issue guidance on the proper nature and extent of consulting work, and individual firms were adapting to managing their own practices in accordance with perceived boundaries of proper conduct.

Competence to perform a given service and the ability to manage it were key factors. Nonattest services offered revenue and provided consultation vital to clients, but they were also an economically attractive way to balance the workload between the tremendous peak experienced around year-end auditing assignments and the underutilization of professionals during the off-peak season.

CONFUSION OVER INDEPENDENCE IN FACT AND APPEARANCE

Writing in the *Accounting Review,* Professor Bernard Greidinger of New York University restated the traditional and uncritical view of independence, in 1951:

> The question of independence, however, is one of *fact* and can be determined only in light of all the pertinent facts in a particular case. . . . The following (examples) represent a brief summary of circumstances which, in specific situations, have been held to be sufficient grounds to disqualify accountants from being *considered* independent in relation to the particular client whose statements they certified.[2]

The failure to distinguish between independence *in fact* and circumstances being *considered a fact,* evidenced in Greidinger's comments, suggest a typical view among accountants not only today but also in this earlier period.

Thus if one asked what constituted a lack of independence in fact, one might be led into a discussion of independence in appearance and vice versa. A short while later the writings of several professionals and an academic study by Mautz and Sharaf (1961) began to clarify the matter. And, as the issue of independence in appearance drew focus, a considerable, and some would later say intractable, debate was initiated.

A CLASSIC DEFINITION OF INDEPENDENCE

In part because he had "grown up" with the issue, John L. Carey, the American Institute's chief staff officer, had witnessed first hand the development of the concerns relating to audit independence. His dedicated efforts to put together a code of CPA conduct led to the publication, in 1947, of his book *Professional Ethics of Public Accounting* and within that text, the following analysis of the *meaning* of independence:

> Independence is an abstract concept, and it is difficult to define either generally or in its peculiar application to the certified public accountant. Essentially it is a state of mind. It is partly synonymous with honesty, integrity, courage, character. It *means,* in simplest terms, that the certified public ac-

---

[2] B. Bernard Greidinger, "When are Independent Public Accountants not in Fact Independent?," *The Accounting Review,* January 1951, pp. 51–52.

countant will tell the truth as he sees it, and will permit no influence, financial or sentimental, to turn him from that course. Everyone will applaud this ideal, but a cynical world requires more than a mere declaration of intention if it is to stake its money on the accountant's word. Therefore, the profession has publicly laid its heaviest penalties on those who breach the unwritten contract of independence, and, in addition, has proscribed specific acts and modes of behavior which might raise a question as to the independence of its members. In other words, the rules do not only provide for punishment of members who are not independent; they also prohibit conduct which might arouse a suspicion of lack of independence. Objective standards of independence have thus been introduced into the code. It is not enough for the member to do what he thinks is right. He must also avoid behavior which could lead to an *inference* that he might be subject to improper influences. The accounting profession must be like Caesar's wife. To be suspected is almost as bad as to be convicted.[3] (Emphasis supplied.)

INDEPENDENCE: A GENERAL AUDITING STANDARD

As postwar stock ownership grew (Table 4) the significance of the public auditor's role increased in social terms; and the concept of independence was even more firmly implanted in the culture of the CPA as auditor with the preparation and subsequent adoption in 1948 of a set of generally accepted auditing standards. This established the preeminence of the audit role for the CPA, and in particular set forth as the second general standard that: "In all matters relating to the assignment, an independence in mental attitude is to be maintained by the auditor or auditors." (These same admonitions as to conduct would be incorporated into early versions of

[3]John L. Carey, *Professional Ethics of Public Accounting*, New York: American Institute of Accountants, 1946, p. 7.

Table 4.   Stock Ownership in the United States: 1952 to 1981

Year	Shareowners	U.S. Population	Percentage
1952	6,490,000	157,553,000	4.1
1956	8,630,000	168,903,000	5.1
1959	12,490,000	177,830,000	7.0
1962	17,010,000	186,538,000	9.1
1965	20,120,000	194,303,000	10.4
1970	30,850,000	205,052,000	15.0
1975	25,270,000	215,973,000	11.7
1980	30,200,000	227,738,000	13.3
1981	32,260,000	230,019,000	14.0

Sources: "U.S. Population," *Economic Report of the President,* Table B-28, Washington, D.C.: GPO, 1985, p. 265. "Stockownership," *Statistical Abstract of the U.S.,* Washington, D.C.: GPO, 1984, p. 524.

Statements on Management Advisory Services 2 and 3[4] issued in 1969 and later withdrawn from the text of *Statements on Standards for Management Advisory Services* (1981).[5])

In the 1948 audit standards document appeared a statement explaining the significance of the second standard and the need to establish "signs" which society could use to recognize independence or the lack thereof, concluding that:

The profession has gradually compiled . . . precepts and conditions to guard against the *presumption* of loss of independence. Presumption is stressed because insofar as intrinsic independence is synonymous with mental integrity, its pos-

[4]American Institute of Certified Public Accountants, Statements on Management Advisory Services No. 2: *Competence in Management Advisory Services,* reprinted in *The Journal of Accountancy,* April 1969, pp. 56–58. American Institute of Certified Public Accountants, Statements on Management Advisory Services No. 3: *Role in Management Advisory Services,* reprinted in *The Journal of Accountancy,* November 1969, pp. 62–65.
[5]American Institute of Certified Public Accountants, *Statements on Standards for Management Advisory Services,* New York: AICPA, 1981.

session is a matter of *personal* quality rather than of rules
that formulate certain objective tests.[6] (Emphasis supplied.)

Even the watershed event of such general standards, however, would not terminate the swirl of discussion about independence—perhaps because, as noted in Greidinger's writing, perceptions of objective and subjective distinctions and
signs thereof had not penetrated the grassroots level of complete understanding. The leadership may have acted and the
literature may have covered the topic with repetition, but
neither an impact on the understanding of professional members nor the general public's awareness were apparent.

Consequently, articles, letters, discussions, and concern over
the issue continued. Writing in 1959, Andrew Barr, Chief
Accountant of the SEC and an important contributor to the
resolution of differences between AICPA and SEC independence positions, observed:

> Recurring questions of surprising frequency demonstrate that
> we have a new generation of accountants in practice today.
> Many of these are not familiar with our rules and have not
> read the history imbedded in our reported cases and sum-
> marized or identified in more accessible form in the Account-
> ing Series Releases.[7]

Barr had properly observed that the influx of veterans and
post-World War II CPAs into the profession had created a
knowledge gap as to independence. The auditor independence issue may have been resolved by one generation to its
satisfaction, but the challenge lay in communicating the essential *meaning* of that resolution to a new and much larger
generation, more diverse in practice and facing new situations which called for interpretations of the fundamental

[6]John L. Carey, *The Rise of the Accounting Profession to Responsibility and Authority:
1937–1969*, vol. 2, New York: AICPA, 1970, p. 179.
[7]Andrew Barr, "The Independent Accountant and the SEC," *The Journal of Accountancy*, October 1959, p. 34.

precept of independence. This same phenomenon would manifest itself on a much greater scale in the 1970s and 1980s, with the important additional complication that the resolution of consulting and professional competition would bring even greater pressure upon the profession's leadership and structure to amend, identify, and relate matters of independence.

THE DUAL STANDARD OF INDEPENDENCE

As the independence standard became identified with CPA auditors, it was a continual reminder that independence was the cornerstone of the profession, a personal attribute of the practitioner. "For if . . . certified public accountant(s) were distrusted individually, they could not be fully trusted as a class."[8] The simple truth of this thought reinforced the idea that independence was the "character" of the CPA and the cornerstone of the profession.

A question which persisted despite the adoption of the general standards of auditing was that a "double standard" of independence existed because of differences between SEC and Institute positions on the matter. Was independence different for CPAs who did not practice before the SEC? Since 1950, the SEC had prohibited *any* direct financial interest by the auditor in the audit client. The AICPA had inserted a qualifier proscribing any *substantial* interest in a client, thereby permitting more discretion on the part of the CPA. The SEC's rule applied to CPAs who audited publicly held companies. The AICPA rule applied to auditors of *any* company, publicly or privately held.

In 1954, the Illinois Society adopted a rule which prohibited members from expressing an opinion on the financial statements of any organization if the member or the mem-

---

[8]"The Practical Aspect of Independence," editorial, *The Journal of Accountancy,* May 1952, p. 549.

ber's partners had a direct or indirect financial interest in an organization. In effect, Illinois was requiring its members to adopt the SEC limits for *all* audits (publicly or closely held). By 1962, the AICPA changed its rules to reflect the position adopted by the SEC and the Illinois Society, resolving one element of the double standard which had developed. It should be recalled that the SEC's first formal independence ruling dated back to 1933, and that nearly 30 years passed before this concept of independence achieved general reconciliation in the profession's view.

INDEPENDENCE: A BASE FOR THE FUTURE

Another element of the "double standard" of independence was noted in *The Ohio CPA Journal* and reported in an editorial in the *Journal of Accountancy*. Was there a different kind of independence for "auditors of companies registered with the SEC and . . . [for] accountants whose practice consisted mainly of services to management, advice and consultation?" In response, the editor commented that:

> Independence is a state of mind, which should prevail in *all the work and all the relations* of a professional certified public accountant. Otherwise, he would subordinate his judgment to that of others and would become only a technical craftsman—abandoning his professional status. On the other hand, lack of independence should not be attributed to an *auditor*, merely because as an *accountant* he renders other services to the same client, unless there is evidence that his state of mind is biased—that he is in fact not independent.[9] (Emphasis supplied.)

[9]John L. Carey, ed., "Independence of Certified Public Accountants," editorial, *The Journal of Accountancy*, February 1949, p. 94. John L. Carey, "The Place of the CPA in Contemporary Society," *The Journal of Accountancy*, September 1958, p. 31.

Writing on the same issue in the following year, Ira Frisbee addressed the question of how far the accountant can go in assisting management with managerial problems and remain independent. He responded:

> Without attempting to discuss fully the entire problem or to [fix] the exact point at which the auditor ceases to be independent, *we may suggest that if his services are advisory only he should be able to maintain even the presumption (as well as the fact) of independence.* If the auditor assumes managerial responsibilities, however, or gives the appearance of doing so, he cannot claim independence in mental attitude and approach in his auditing work.[10] (Emphasis supplied.)

With these remarks the profession's posture was being formed as to CPA consulting "independence," in fact and in appearance.

By 1962, when the AICPA membership adopted Rule 1.01 as a part of the professional code of ethics, there was substantial conformity between the AICPA position and the SEC position. Independence in fact was emphasized, but the new ethical rule acknowledged that certain circumstances resulted in CPAs being considered not independent—the "appearance element." However, no mention of consulting services as giving rise to an independence conflict was included among such circumstances.

Perhaps the earliest codified use of both of the explicit distinguishing terms *independence in fact* and *independence in appearance* occurred in 1974 when, in SEC Accounting Series Release 165, the Commission stated that:

> It is essential that both the fact and the appearance of independence be sustained so that the confidence of the investing public in the reliability of audited financial statements and

---

[10]Ira N. Frisbee, "How Personal Attributes of the Auditor Affect the Application of Auditing Standards," *The Journal of Accountancy*, February 1950, p. 123.

the integrity of the public accounting profession will be maintained and enhanced.[11]

At approximately the same time, the AICPA had again revised its rules of conduct (March 1, 1973) and incorporated therein certain interpretations of the previous rules of conduct—including Interpretation 101.3 on Accounting Services, which emphasized independence in appearance, noting that the auditor should consider whether he or she is "lacking in independence in the eyes of a reasonable observer."[12]

Therefore, by the mid-1970s, the concept of independence in appearance had been articulated in the SEC releases, and the concept of the "reasonable observer" judging the issue of independence relative to accounting services had been introduced into the rules of conduct of the AICPA. Within these a basis for an independence expectation in CPA non-audit roles had been set forth.

CONSULTING COMES OF AGE IN THE CPA PROFESSION

In the fall of 1953 the American Institute's first committee on management services by CPAs was formed. The initial objective of this committee was to encourage local accounting firms to extend their practices into areas already explored by the larger firms. For example, from 1947 until his retirement, John McEachren provided the leadership for Touche Ross in developing management services.[13] At Price Waterhouse, management advisory services were the responsibility

[11]U.S. Securities and Exchange Commission, "Notice of Amendments to Require Increased Disclosure of Relationships Between Registrants and Their Independent Public Accountants," ASR No. 165 (December 20, 1974), in *Accounting Series Releases and Staff Accounting Bulletins*, Chicago: Commerce Clearing House, June 1, 1981, p. 3315.

[12]American Institute of Certified Public Accountants, *AICPA Professional Standards (vol. B): Accounting and Review Services, Ethics Bylaws, International Accounting, International Auditing, Management Advisory Services, Quality Control, Tax Practice*, sec. ET 101.04, Chicago: Commerce Clearing House, June 1, 1984, p. 4413.

[13]Touche Ross & Co., "Touche Ross: A Biography," *Tempo*, Special 25th Anniversary Issue, 1972, p. 39.

of Joseph Pelej.[14] At Arthur Andersen, an administrative services division was in place after the end of World War II.[15] At Peat Marwick, William Black hired Frank Wallace from McKinsey & Co. to direct an expanding scope of services, and pointed out that the firm had been doing consulting work at the turn of the century.[16] At Deloitte Haskins & Sells, the task fell to Everett Shifflett to organize management advisory services.[17]

The issue of the propriety of a broader scope of services per se, including MAS (management advisory services), was not so much the concern since practitioners in large and small firms alike pointed to their traditional involvement as justification for continuation. The issue was more what *range* of services firms could provide within the framework of their competence and supervisory capability, and at the same time give recognition to economic feasibility in a market where every manner of non-CPA was also competing for engagements.

THE ECONOMICS OF CONSULTING

Paul Grady wrote in 1945 that:

> The curse of public accounting in the past has been the tremendous stress and strain on all personnel during the first quarter of the year, accompanied by the large numbers of temporary workers . . . the basic causes of the old peak season are still with us and they must be conquered as a condition precedent to satisfactory progress by the profession.[18]

[14]John B. Inglis, *My Life and Times*, Passaic, N.J.: George Dixon, 1974, p. 131.
[15]Arthur Andersen & Co., *The First Fifty Years: 1913–1963*, Chicago: Arthur Andersen & Co., 1963, p. 94.
[16]T.A. Wise, *Peat, Marwick, Mitchell & Co.: 85 Years*, New York: Peat, Marwick, Mitchell & Co., 1982, p. 49.
[17]Haskins & Sells, *Haskins & Sells—Our First Seventy-Five Years*, New York: Haskins & Sells, 1970, p. 142.
[18]Paul Grady, *Written Contributions of Selected Accounting Practitioners*, vol. 2, ed., V.K. Zimmerman, Urbana, IL: Center for International Education and Research in Accounting, 1978, p. 163.

An important initial economic justification for the CPA to offer advisory services was found in the need to overcome the problems of peak seasonality of established CPA service lines—particularly auditing. Unlike the old line coal company which balanced its winter business by selling ice in the summer, CPA firms' talent was likely to be unused after audit and tax season. One means of stabilizing this strategic professional resource was by developing the consulting practice. And the larger the year-end audit practice grew (companies seemed to continue to favor a calendar year-end despite attempts by CPAs and others to foster the so-called natural business year), the greater the talent component, which in turn needed to be put to productive work the rest of the year or be summarily dismissed.

Unless a permanent form of employment could be developed, top college-educated recruits for the profession could be easily attracted to more permanent and secure positions in business and government. Without the best talent, the CPA profession ran the risk of being unable to respond with the calibre of service needed to meet client demands. The peak season could no longer be managed as it had in the past—and the consulting service role seemed to help resolve the imbalance. While much would be done—via technology, time banking, and interim review and reporting work—to level out the pressure of the auditing season, the calendar for auditing and tax activity still dictated a "busy season" followed by a slack period.

THE INSTITUTIONAL RESPONSE TO CPA CONSULTING

As the new Institute committee got underway it was charged with the task of finding answers to a number of key questions: "What consulting services is a CPA generally equipped to render?" "What special preparation might be required to enable him or her to render such services?" "What are the areas of management decisions to which accounting relates?"

"Should management services be divorced from those commonly identified as accounting services?" "Should they be merged?"

The 1953 edition of the *CPA Handbook* included a chapter by Marquis Eaton (soon to be a president of the American Institute), entitled "The CPA as a Business Consultant." It contained listings of functional distinctions to guide organizations developing advisory services and summarized the types of engagements currently being fulfilled by CPA advisors. The chapter was a "nuts and bolts" guide to the factors businesses used in choosing a consultant, which the major non-CPA consulting firms were, and books and articles on subjects related to consulting.[19]

By 1957 the Institute had prepared and distributed a pamphlet describing the management services offerings of a CPA. This report of the "Wellington Committee" also included a descriptive meaning for management services and an eight-part listing of service areas: general management, finance, production, sales, office management, purchasing, traffic and transportation, and personnel. The committee also began to issue bulletins and other materials to assist practitioners in addressing their responsibilities in these areas.[20]

Management consulting was becoming, in the words of a local practice member of the Institute, "the third dimension of accounting."[21] A factor influencing the scope of consulting services, was, of course, frequent competition with non-CPAs who were not limited in their advertising and were not constrained to observe the rules of conduct of AICPA members.

Writing on the subject of professional ethics and public

[19]Marquis G. Eaton, "The CPA as a Business Consultant," Chapter 25 in *The CPA Handbook,* New York: American Institute of Accountants, 1954.
[20]Carey, *The Rise of the Accounting Profession,* pp. 363–64. Roger Wellington, "Management Services—A Challenge to the Profession," *The Journal of Accountancy,* October 1957, pp. 54–58. James Don Edwards, *History of Public Accounting in the United States,* 1960, reprint, University, Alabama: The University of Alabama Press, 1978, p. 207.
[21]Albert Christen, "Advisory Service to Business: Its Rewards and Hazards," *The Journal of Accountancy,* April 1954, p. 464.

opinion in 1958, Thomas Higgins, senior partner of Arthur Young, noted that:

> There is no unanimity of thought among accountants as to the boundary line to which the practice of accounting stops in management services.

He also said:

> The ethics committee . . . proposed a new rule of ethics which in effect stated that a member should not undertake professional services unless he or a member of his firm was competent, as evidenced by training or experience, to perform or supervise such services. [This first attempt was] dropped, however, because of strenuous objections by a great many accountants throughout the country. . . .[22]

Higgins also articulated early recognition of the current constraint in providing advisory services—that the accountant should avoid any *decision-making* role. He said:

> [A] CPA can keep his position of independence [while providing management services], provided he keeps his relationship, as he should, at the advisory level as distinct from the decision-making or operating level.

In response to the inquiry as to whether, by setting up a separate service bureau to provide certain mechanized functions, a CPA-operator could avoid ethical problems, Higgins stated:

> The ethics committee has been definite as to all such queries, taking the position that the Institute's code must apply to all the professional activities of members practicing the profession regardless of competition from non-CPAs and that any

---

[22]Thomas G. Higgins, "Professional Ethics and Public Opinion," *The Journal of Accountancy,* November 1958, p. 36.

efforts to divert the field of management services to an organization which would be beyond the rules of conduct would be improper.[23]

SOME ACADEMIC VIEWS

The position that CPA independence applied to all services had been championed by many others, including academics, one of whom, writing in 1954, stated that it was "indispensable to the profession that the concept of independence be not restricted to public auditing."[24]

CPA interest in expanding the scope of services was complemented by findings from a dissertation research project completed in 1959 at Harvard. The study, "Professional Standards for Management Consulting in the United States," found that:

(a) The public accounting profession belongs in the consulting field.

(b) Its audit relationship with clients offers distinct advantages to both CPA and client in the consulting area.

(c) If approached and carried out properly, the management consulting field could ultimately be taken over, or at least dominated by the public accounting profession.

(d) The professional structure to accomplish . . . [MAS] . . . already exists.

(e) The CPA is an established professional . . . [and has] . . . a professional attitude and a commitment to live up to explicit professional rules.

(f) . . . the user of consulting services will be safer in placing his management problem in the hands of a qualified CPA.[25]

[23]Higgins, "Professional Ethics," p. 37.
[24]G.D. Brighton, "Aid to Management Beyond the Audit," *The Accounting Review,* October 1954, p. 589.
[25]A.W. Patrick and C.L. Quittmeyer, "The CPA and Management Services," *The Accounting Review,* January 1963, p. 117.

COUNCIL RECOGNITION

In 1969 the Council of the Institute adopted a resolution which stated, "It is an objective of the Institute, recognizing that management services are a proper function of CPAs, to encourage all CPAs to perform the entire range of management services consistent with their professional competence, ethical standards and responsibility.[26]

The SEC, however, was also beginning to take an interest in the increasing attention the CPA profession was placing on management services. The 1957 annual report of the Commission contained a warning with respect to independence and management services. The Commission noted:

> Another reason for finding a lack of independence . . . is the fact that accountants intending to certify financial statements included in such filings have been interested in serving the client's management, or in some cases large stockholders, in several capacities and in doing so have not taken care to maintain a clear distinction between giving advice to management and service as personal representatives of management or owners and making business decisions for them.[27]

At what point does the decision-making process begin and end? Writing in 1962 in response to this question Professor Moss noted:

> This confusion can be dispelled by dissecting the decision-making process into three parts:
> (1) Determining the problem.
> (2) Discovering alternative courses of action.
> (3) Selecting that course of action which will lead to the profit objective of the firm.

[26]*The CPA*, February 1961, p. 2.
[27]"SEC Comments on Independence with Respect to CPAs," *The Journal of Accountancy*, April 1958, p. 77.

The independent CPA can and should aid management in the first two phases of the decision process. . . . however, when the action step, the act of choosing is performed . . . such is a responsibility of the manager.[28]

THE CORE OF CPA CONCERNS

The principal ethical issues related to consulting and independence at this point, therefore, were turning out to be: (1) competence, (2) supervision, and (3) discriminating between consulting (advising) and deciding or choosing among alternatives. Another issue, that of "unfair advantage," raised by non-CPA consultants, would be brought more into focus during the congressional oversight hearings in the next decade.

The claim of CPAs for right of confidentiality (between the professional and the client) was also to be raised, but it was not addressed in an advisory context, but in the context of an attest engagement.

Competition with nonaccountants in the market for management consulting (a market which *Fortune* magazine had estimated in 1955 to be generating gross fees of $4 million) was introducing accountants to the need to find a new balance between their professional character and keen competitive instincts.[29] Non-CPAs were not restricted in their advertising nor were they bound by rules of conduct affecting CPAs. But while the CPA may have initially felt encumbered by ethics, there was a rationale for these checks on behavior, which Wilcox explained as follows:

> Some part of the accountant's independence is inevitably lost when he emerges from an undignified scramble for an en-

[28]Morton F. Moss, "Management Services and the CPA Examination," *The Accounting Review,* October 1962, p. 733.
[29]Thomas W. Leland, "Helping the Small Client With His Budget Problems," *The Journal of Accountancy,* October 1955, p. 57.

gagement. His prestige—and his ability to obtain acceptance of his recommendations—have been diminished.[30]

A few absolute limits to consulting practice, however, did begin to appear. As a *Journal* editorial in January 1956, pointed out:

> To give investment advice in connection with the purchase of a business where the experience and knowledge of the accountant are pertinent to the facts of the case, involves no loss of independent professional status for a CPA, whereas setting himself up as a general investment counselor would obviously be improper.[31]

The attitude of the era was summed up by a practitioner who stated: "The conclusion seems inescapable that if management services are performed by CPAs, all of our rules of conduct are applicable."[32]

SUMMARY

The CPA was charged with accepting the responsibility of professionalism while addressing a new era of high potential both for personal reward and general social and economic benefit. The professional literature and the professional leadership committed themselves to a rigorous posture insisting that ethical responsibilities went with the CPA wherever the services were.

"Who," asked Carey, "would engage a doctor or lawyer or a certified public accountant who was known to put personal

---

[30]Edward B. Wilcox, "Ethics: The Profession on Trial," *The Journal of Accountancy,* November 1955, p. 74.

[31]John Lawler, "Management Services and Independence," *The Journal of Accountancy,* January 1956, p. 28.

[32]Ira N. Frisbee, "Ethical Considerations in Rendering Management Services," *The Journal of Accountancy,* March 1957, p. 30.

rewards ahead of service to his patient or client?"[33] In the golden age of post-World War II America, the answer was obvious. The good guys did what was right. But times were indeed changing and a hint of understanding about the candor needed for these times is found in the article by a noted practitioner, Ira Frisbee:

> On the question of maintaining independence in auditing work for a client who regularly receives the accountant's advice upon management problems or for whom various other management services are rendered, it is probable that all doubts as to complete independence cannot be avoided.[34]

Here at least was the statement of the issue of "degree." How complete must independence be? Was it humanly possible to avoid bias and exist within such a vacuum? How did a generation of accountants plot a reasonable and socially purposeful destiny? And, more important, what elements should be part of the character of the emerging multiservice CPA professional? Would complete independence be the rhetoric of both government agencies and professional groups?

[33]John L. Carey, "Professional Ethics and the Public Interest," *The Journal of Accountancy*, November 1956, p. 38.
[34]Frisbee, "Ethical Consideration," p. 33.

5

A Search for Compatibility of Services

1962 TO 1976

The notion that the goal of the professional accountant is public or social service is nonsense. His function is to provide the best possible service to his specific clients, the people who pay for his efforts. And in doing this his attitude is not one of independence or aloofness; instead he should be endeavoring to become as fully acquainted as practicable with each client's affairs and problems and be prepared to give constructive advice on his internal accounting methods and all phases of financial measurement, review, and planning. . . . Of course, this doesn't imply that the accountant should condone or participate in any kind of crooked or destructive techniques. . . . This point would be taken care of by emphasizing competence and integrity rather than independence and public service.[1]

William A. Paton, 1971

[1]William A. Paton, "Earmarks of a Profession—and the APB," *The Journal of Accountancy*, January 1971, p. 41.

*If the accountant approaches the audit with a predisposition—
whether conscious or otherwise—to validate management's work
rather than subject it to careful scrutiny, public confidence in
business and the profession will be decreased and audits will be
useless.*[2]

Harold Williams, 1977

[2]Harold Williams, statement to U.S. Congress, Senate, Subcommittee
on Reports, Accounting and Management of the Committee on Governmental Affairs, "Improving the Accountability of Publicly Owned
Corporations and Their Auditors," 95th Congress, 1st Session, November 1977, New York: Haskins & Sells, p. 5.

What Professor Paton, the dean of accounting professors, overlooks is that the term "independence" is imbedded in the legislation and the literature of the profession; it cannot be wished away easily or fully substituted by other words. What Williams, formerly dean of the UCLA Management School and former chairman of the SEC, overlooks is the truth of Professor Paton's observation—that the public is a faceless and unspecified audience. Often when the public well-being is involved, responsibility for it has been assumed by a profession which in turn exercises both a right and a responsibility to conduct itself in an altruistic fashion. A common alternative to a profession providing such service to society is for the service to be assumed by government in the name of the public.

It is within the limits of these views that the profession's aspirations to provide a broader field of service by which to use its talents will have to be decided. Independence will remain an issue, as will the issue of responsibility to society; what will require resolution are the respective roles which the profession and the government will play in providing a necessary and valuable service.

The 1964 amendments to the Securities Exchange Act had the practical effect of requiring an even larger number of publicly held companies—those traded over the counter—to submit annually audited reports to the SEC. And with the growth of the new securities offerings during the "go-go years" of the 1960s, registration work also continued to provide ample opportunities for accounting firms to expand both in size and in public stature.

The CPA profession had achieved a recognized level of credibility—accorded by sociologists the status of an "established" profession. CPAs found themselves in the company of older, recognized professions listed in a study published in the *American Journal of Sociology*.[3] American Institute mem-

---

[3]Harold L. Wilensky, "The Professionalization of Everyone?," *The American Journal of Sociology*, September 1964, p. 143.

bership, numbering slightly less than 45,000 in 1962, would
increase to over 121,000 by 1976 (see Table 1, Introduction).
The transformation of the profession in this period would
strain every resource—leadership, experience, education, and
tradition.

A STRATEGIC OUTLOOK FOR THE CPA PROFESSION

A principal challenge in this transformation was the establishment and implementation of a long-range plan. In 1962,
the Institute's long-range planning committee released a study
entitled *The Accounting Profession—Where Is It Headed?* This
committee report identified the attest function, tax practice,
and consulting as the profession's scope of service for the
future. By such a strategic orientation, the profession had
signaled its general level of commitment to society. But within
the particular scope of services for consulting per se, the
report offered less guidance. "What the profession has needed,"
it said, "is a logical statement describing the area of management in which CPAs generally can render useful services,
and how these services are naturally integrated with the familiar and regular work of the accounting profession."[4]

It is in quest of this "logical statement" that members of
the profession, the public, and critics alike would expend
much energy during the period preceding the series of
congressional inquiries which challenged the so-called accounting establishment in the late 1970s.

How to determine the range of consulting services became
a burning issue. What professional and social concerns required attention? How would the structure of the profession
and the administration of practice be impacted? What educational and testing requirements should be considered? All
of these questions needed to be addressed.

[4]John L. Carey, ed., *The Accounting Profession: Where Is It Headed?*, New York: AICPA,
1962, p. 77.

MANAGING THE CONSULTING FUNCTION

If the profession had established consulting as a legitimate area of professional service, and if this was legitimate (a field not precluded by medicine, law, or engineering, for example), then the issue was no longer whether CPAs should undertake consulting work but rather *how to manage it.*

On this issue, suggestions, criticisms, studies, and opinions were to abound. During the decade and a half discussed in this chapter, the cauldron of debate simmered, heated, and finally overflowed—and what remained was a unique brew, strongly seasoned with the conservatism of CPA auditors who had long directed the affairs of the profession, and buoyed by the opportunism of the waves of young college-educated CPAs eager to stake their claim.

Among the concerns expressed about the process of managing the scope of advisory services was the possible conflict of interest when the CPA also was fulfilling his or her duties as a public-company auditor. The first widely publicized discussion of this matter appeared in a monograph, *The Philosophy of Auditing,* by R.K. Mautz and Hussein A. Sharaf, published by the American Accounting Association in 1961. The authors held that management advisory services (and tax services) tended to cloud the *appearance* of independence as it related to CPA auditors. And they recommended that the audit function be separately managed from other types of services offered by accounting firms.[5]

The academic community followed up on these suggestions, often to the dismay of practitioners who felt the suggestions and the analysis were not in accord with reality. Academics conducted and reported on surveys which suggested that a significant number of members of the financial community were concerned about the possible conflict as CPAs filled dual roles as auditors and as consultants. Briloff, whose

[5]R.K. Mautz and Hussein A. Sharaf, *The Philosophy of Auditing,* Madison, WI: American Accounting Association, 1961, pp. 218 ff.

doctoral research had criticized CPAs' justifications for consulting, also questioned whether the CPA profession had not reached the limits of presumptuousness by preparing to offer a mix of services for which educational preparation had not been established. This raised the issue of *competence,* rather than focusing directly on any potential conflict.[6]

Professor Briloff, however, was equally critical of CPA firms and their posture regarding perceived consulting-auditing independence conflicts. He asserted that there was no countervailing institutional measure affording the profession a "test of review" for the performance of consulting services in the same way the SEC afforded such review in the case of audits of public companies, and the IRS afforded in the tax field.[7] This notion of "test of review" had been discussed earlier in the literature in an article by Robert Trueblood of Touche Ross & Co. in the *Journal* in 1962.[8] Thus was anticipated by 15 or more years the profession's imposition of "peer reviews" (first of firms' accounting and audit practices and then, gradually, to include a review of consulting engagements to test for compliance with applicable independence standards) with the formation of the AICPA's Division for CPA firms in the late 1970s. This concept is more fully discussed later in the chapter.

CONSULTING SERVICE GUIDELINES

As one practitioner put it, "In management services and systems work there is little or no authority to refer to, no crutch

---

[6]Abraham J. Briloff, "Old Myths and New Realities in Accountancy," *The Accounting Review,* July 1966, p. 495.
[7]Abraham J. Briloff, *The Effectiveness of Accounting Communication,* Ph.D. dissertation, New York University, 1965, p. 227.
[8]Robert M. Trueblood, "The Management Service Function in Public Accounting," *The Journal of Accountancy,* July 1961, p. 43.

to lean on. *We are alone.* This is what I . . . call the 'moment of truth' in management services."[9]

It was becoming accepted by professionals and expected by others that in "all phases of his work, the CPA would exhibit the type of self-reliant professional independence which is essential to all professionals."[10] This was a given, but the question remained how to implement the concept to ensure maintenance of independence in audit work where consulting services were needed.

A direct and draconian answer would be to ban auditors from doing consulting work for attest clients—permitting consulting work only for nonattest clients. This has been suggested because of a perception that there is an "inherent" conflict between the two services. Such a conflict, it could therefore be argued, transcends the operation of any rules that might be devised.

If there is an "inherent" conflict, however, whether a client is a public or a private corporation is not relevant, and any prohibition perceived to be necessary must be invoked against large and small CPA practice units alike. All offer a mix of attest and consulting services to business at various levels (see Table 7, Chapter 6). Such a prohibition, opponents argue, would single out and penalize small practitioners who have a limited number of (or no) public clients. It also would reduce the availability of a valuable resource—the CPA consultant—especially in small communities where small businesses could ill afford the higher cost of separation of attest and consulting services. Furthermore, some form of attest services still is essential to banks or for credit granting purposes.

[9]Lee Engle, "The Moment of Truth in Management Services," *The Journal of Accountancy,* February 1969, p. 33.
[10]John L. Carey and William O. Doherty, "The Concept of Independence—Review and Restatement," *The Journal of Accountancy,* January 1966, p. 38.

IN SEARCH OF EVIDENCE

Was the "inherent conflict" readily demonstrable or was it less real than imagined? An early effort to determine this was made by the AICPA's Ad Hoc Committee on Independence (the Devore Committee). In 1969, the final report of that committee stated that, among 44 state boards of accountancy responding to an inquiry whether they had ever taken disciplinary action regarding asserted lack of independence in cases involving consulting service, none reported ever having had such a case.[11]

Leading practitioners who sought to deal with the issue noted that CPAs had provided millions of hours of management advisory services to their clients. Extensive inquiries by the Ad Hoc Committee, the SEC, and critics failed to bring to light confirmed cases of conflict between audit services and advisory services—although instances would later be alleged in several cases, including Westec and Dupont Securities.

In addition, the AICPA's Commission on Auditors' Responsibilities, formed in the early 1970s to assess the changing role of the CPA-auditor, directly addressed the independence issue. The Commission sought evidence bearing on independence and the consulting function. "The commission," *Business Week* reported, "uncovered no evidence that management consulting by CPA firms compromised the auditor's independence."[12] But the Commission also warned that *potential* conflicts are very real.

Therefore, while it was recognized that not all alleged audit failure-consulting relationships were known, there appeared to be a striking lack of factual basis on which to launch a prohibition against providing attest and consulting services for the same client. Finally, in recognition of the need for a

---

[11]American Institute of Certified Public Accountants, "Final Report of Ad Hoc Committee on Independence," October 3, 1969, reprinted in *The Journal of Accountancy*, December 1969, p. 51.

[12]"A Sharper Definition of the Auditor's Job," *Business Week*, March 28, 1977, p. 56.

rational rather than an emotional response to a "problem" the existence of which lacked sound evidential support, many argued that a consideration of *inherent* conflict itself must have some foundation and that it should be based on a perception of independence which requires a degree of attainment meeting the test of reasonableness. To summarize one position: No professional is free from personal and professional preferences or biases, and no service can be rendered without concentrated contact with client personnel; no consultant or auditor is so automatic in his or her duties that he or she will ever be perfectly independent.[13]

Other academics indirectly challenged views of the profession's critics. One in particular, writing in July 1963, stated that the entire field was changing:

> There are signs on the horizon that management consulting firms, data processing and reporting organizations and other comparable organizations are already preparing themselves to expand their services in the data attest area. [So] the profession needs immediate action in focusing the objectives of professional accounting more closely on matters that lie at the very heart of the management process.[14]

Professor Titard, reporting the results of his survey research on independence and consulting in 1971, found that the objection to CPAs rendering management services dropped sharply when there was a provision that the CPA firm would "manage" the services by separately administering the functions of audit and management services.[15]

The inherent conflict/direct prohibition scheme, therefore, was suspect and might indeed deny strategic services to all

[13]Felix Kaufman, "Professional Consulting by CPAs," *The Accounting Review*, October 1967, p. 719.
[14]William L. Campfield, "Critical Paths for Professional Accountants During the New Management Revolution," *The Accounting Review*, July 1963, p. 522.
[15]Pierre L. Titard, "Independence and MAS—Opinions of Financial Statement Users," *The Journal of Accountancy*, July 1971, p. 51.

levels of the economy. An alternative was to recognize that the process should be left to the markets and professional groups to manage, with more *emphasis* on education and self-regulation.

DIFFERENT MEANINGS OF INDEPENDENCE

Confusing the issue were the various meanings which interested parties attached to the word "independence," often with their own agendas in mind. Professors Carmichael and Swieringa, writing in 1968, warned therefore that care must be taken not to misconstrue professional independence (self-reliance and nonsubordination of professional opinion), auditor independence (freedom from bias or objectivity in forming delicate judgments), and perceived independence (that quality which is impaired when a situation suggests a conflict of interest to a reasonable observer who has knowledge of all the facts).[16]

A more pragmatic approach was taken by a practitioner writing in 1963. He asked: "Can the financial pressure to retain a client affect an auditor's independence?" It could, he believed, but he further observed that that pressure exists whether or not the CPA functions also as a consultant. It (the pressure) is not greatly increased by the addition of consulting fees to auditing fees. Consulting fees, the writer pointed out, while they may be substantial, tend to be nonrecurring. The audit fees are bound to be more important to the accounting firm in the long run. One would be reluctant to jeopardize an "annuity" arrangement for the price of a single contract. He concluded: "A poor consulting job may, indeed, risk the loss of an audit engagement, but it is a pressure for

---

[16]D.R. Carmichael and R.J. Swieringa, "The Compatibility of Auditing Independence and Management Services—An Identification of Issues," *The Accounting Review*, October 1968, pp. 697–705.

consulting quality and for consultant independence, not a
pressure against audit independence."[17]

COMPATIBILITY

Still another view on the management of the consulting function was offered by Professor Walter Kell, writing in 1968:

> In performing the full range of management services, a CPA
> engages in two fundamentally different types of service: (1)
> accounting services related to the client's total information
> system and (2) administrative services that extend beyond the
> traditional boundaries of accounting.[18]

Kell contended that accounting services were compatible with
both independence in fact and independence in appearance.
However, he considered administrative services to be incompatible with independence in appearance since these services
tend to associate the CPA more closely with the management
process. Kell does not explicitly explain the "traditional
boundaries" of accounting, but he seems to be defining an
appropriate scope of services as one limited to dealing with
"information."

George S. Olive, writing for the *Journal* in 1969, noted
similarly that there were "limits" to consulting services: "We
feel that for the present at least, our management services
work should be accounting related. We are not experts at
plant layout or setting labor standards. . . ."[19]

The AICPA Ad Hoc Committee mentioned previously also
noted the view of Eric Kohler, an elder statesman of the

[17]Kenneth S. Axelson, "Are Consulting and Auditing Compatible?," *The Journal of
Accountancy,* April 1963, pp. 55, 57.
[18]Walter G. Kell, "Public Accounting's Irresistible Force and Immovable Object,"
The Accounting Review, April 1968, p. 273.
[19]George S. Olive, Jr., "Management Services—a Local Firm Approach," *The Journal
of Accountancy,* April 1960, p. 33.

profession, on the subject of services to management. Kohler held that a public accountant's established services to management included "preparation of income tax returns or aid in their preparation or review. . . . [b]udgetary procedures, costing methods, pension schemes . . . [all are] natural consequences of the auditor's developed skills." Kohler, however, cautioned against services such as "market surveys, factory layout, psychological testing or public opinion polls . . . as well as executive recruitment for a fee. . . ."[20]

Colin Brummet, a young CPA staff accountant writing at about the same time, viewed the issue differently—that services remote from accounting are precisely those least calculated to give rise to any real or imagined conflicts. In contrast to Kohler's views, he stated:

> Some types of management advisory services—for example, psychological testing, public opinion polls, executive recruitment and market surveys are sufficiently far removed from the audit function that there is little likelihood that the auditor's independence would be jeopardized.[21]

ESTABLISHING A RANGE OF SERVICES: COMPETENCE AND INDEPENDENCE ISSUES

Resolving the limits of a range of services for the CPA-consultant is related not only to independence but to competence as well, because of the potential variety of knowledge, skills, and abilities which could be deemed compatible with established CPA practice. If consulting skill requirements extended beyond or were inconsistent with traditional skills used to support the principal or franchised (audit) services, how would appropriate supervision, education, testing, and

[20]American Institute of Certified Public Accountants, "Final Report of Ad Hoc Committee on Independence," p. 53.
[21]Colin K. Brummet, "Management Advisory Services: A Matter of Image," *The Journal of Accountancy*, May 1971, p. 66.

licensing procedures operate to ensure that competency was achieved and maintained within the institutions of the CPA profession? If required consulting competencies were inconsistent with audit competences, would established education and testing processes be sufficient to ensure consistent quality and comparable supervision within CPAs' professional ranks?

This, in turn, raises a question whether the entire range of a defined scope of services must be delivered by a large firm with separate staffs for each, or as well by a smaller firm with the same individuals fulfilling a variety of professional roles.

ACADEMIC AMBIVALENCE

The involvement of the academic community in the independence debate was often stimulating yet sometimes disappointing, particularly if a study wandered into esoteric concerns. One group of academics who studied the behavioral interplay between client pressures and auditor power (i.e., ability to maintain independence, however defined) concluded that most consulting activities, being nonroutine and of direct benefit to the client, *increased* the independence of the auditor and the auditor's "power" over the client since the auditor provided a needed service of value.[22]

Other academics argued that such behavioral models were naive or that the evidence related thereto was insufficient to support or reject such contentions. Still others surveyed attitudes about SEC and AICPA positions on independence rulings and suggested that: "On the whole it appears that the SEC's rulings on independence are more conservative than necessary . . . [whereas] . . . the AICPA rulings are much closer to . . . user opinions."[23]

[22]Stephen E. Loeb, "The Auditor-Firm Conflict of Interests: Its Implications for Independence: A Comment," *The Accounting Review*, October 1975, p. 844.
[23]David Lavin, "Perceptions of the Independence of the Auditor," *The Accounting Review*, January 1976, p. 49.

A final trio of academic contributors suggested that the issue revolved about a "structuring" of the decision process such that the CPA remained independent even while performing all the steps of a complex decision process—except the final step, which requires computing the expected value of each act and selecting the act with the highest value. This last step could only be taken by management, and if the "consultant" took it, he or she crossed that necessary line between advice and action and would sacrifice independence and objectivity.[24]

During 1972, Professors Timothy Ross and Ronald Hartley reported the results of their consulting/independence survey, as did Professor Pierre Titard. The former pair found that a majority of their respondents did not question whether a CPA firm could appropriately perform consulting services for an audit client and still maintain audit independence. Titard's survey also found that the appearance of independence is not a serious problem for the profession, based on his survey of 223 representatives of the financial community. What was of interest was that two particular types of service—mergers and business acquisitions, and executive recruitment—placed highest on the list of types of services which executives and analysts thought should be prohibited to CPA firms, even if different audit and consulting personnel were involved in the consulting engagement.[25] These surveys would seem to suggest that the CPA was justified in the view that general consulting services were compatible with simultaneous performance of attest services for the same client, with but two clear exceptions.

Practitioners continued to reflect on the basis of the public's perception of conflict. William Seidman, writing in 1972, noted:

[24]James Wesley Deskins, "Management Services and Management Decisions," *The Journal of Accountancy*, January 1965, pp. 50–54.
[25]Ronald V. Hartley and Timothy L. Ross, "MAS and Audit Independence: An Image Problem," *The Journal of Accountancy*, November 1972, pp. 42–51. Titard, "Independence and MAS," p. 51.

For years accountants have been performing the three A's of service: the Attest function (audit), the Advisory function (management and accounting advisory services), the Advocacy function (primarily tax). Questions revolve not around whether the accountant is independent but whether, in terms of today's macro audience's receiving instant but capsulated communications, the message will be *believable*.[26]

INSTITUTIONAL RESPONSES

While academics, critics, and practitioners wrestled with the issues of scope and range of consulting, and how to manage the process of delivering those services, institutional forces began to rationalize the strategic place of consultancy among the proper service roles for CPAs.

The AICPA commissioned a study to establish what CPA consultants do, how they acquire requisite knowledge, and whether such knowledge could be tested as a basis for peer validation of qualifications. The study, entitled MASBOKE (MAS Body of Knowledge and Examination), was begun in 1974 and completed in 1976. It concluded that there was indeed an identifiable body of knowledge for MAS and that it would be feasible to base qualifying examinations on that knowledge.[27]

In 1969 the Institute also released three nonbinding *Statements on Management Advisory Services* to assist practitioners in identifying the principles of management of MAS practice and elements of competence necessary to provide professional service. These general standards set forth descriptions of the:

---

[26]L. William Seidman, "The End of the Great Green Eyeshade," *The Journal of Accountancy,* January 1972, p. 53.

[27]Wallace E. Olson, *The Accounting Profession; Years of Trial: 1969–1980,* New York: AICPA, 1982, p. 199. Edward L. Summers and Kenneth E. Knight, "The AICPA Studies MAS in CPA Firms," *The Journal of Accountancy,* March 1975, pp. 56–64.

1. Nature of management advisory services by independent accounting firms

2. Competency expected in management advisory services

3. Role of the CPA in providing management advisory services[28]

By 1974 the Institute had also initiated an Annual MAS Conference in an effort to provide CPA consulting practitioners a recurring forum through which to exchange ideas and hold discussions of relevant opportunities and issues. The conference has continued to draw important support from practitioners and has afforded a source of identification beyond the firm practice unit for CPA specialists in consulting.

A NEW ETHICAL PATTERN—A ROLE FOR THE INFORMED, REASONABLE OBSERVER

During the 1970s, the Institute modified the position relating to the matter of independence and consulting. In the restatement of the Code of Ethics which became effective in March 1973, the need for concern over the appearance of independence as related to consulting was changed from the previous treatment under the old rules. In explaining the change, Thomas Higgins and Wallace Olson, writing in the *Journal of Accountancy* (March 1972), detailed the structure of the new code of conduct as containing three distinct sections: first, an essay containing the philosophical concepts; next, a rule, infraction of which would make a member subject to disciplinary action; and, finally, an interpretation filling the place of previous "opinions."

---

[28]American Institute of Certified Public Accountants, *Statements on Standards for Management Advisory Services,* New York: AICPA, February 1969.

As to consulting and independence, the authors of the new rules then inquire:

> How important is the *appearance* of independence in the case of management advisory services and tax practice? The *essay* section states that while a CPA need not *appear* to be independent in performing such services, it is desirable that he avoid the relationships proscribed in Rule 1.01 (direct financial interest and employment proscriptions).[29] (Emphasis supplied.)

In the "interpretation" section, however, one then finds reference to the need for the auditors to be "concerned" about independence in appearance per se by suggesting that they consider whether they are lacking in independence in the eyes of a reasonable observer.

TEST OF REVIEW

Perhaps the most telling institutional commitment to the issue of consulting and independence during the period, however, was found in the quality of the individuals and the involvement of the leadership in discussing the issue. Rarely, apart from the issue of setting reporting standards, had so much energy been so publicly focused on a subject as it was on the management of consulting and professional independence.

As a result of the commitment of such talent, sound concerns, constructive self-criticism and hopeful developments were forthcoming. For example, Higgins agreed that:

> There is a danger in management advisory services, but it does not negate the consultant's independence. This danger arises when management, misunderstanding the proper role

---

[29]Thomas G. Higgins and Wallace E. Olson, "Restating the Ethics Code: A Decision for the Times," *The Journal of Accountancy*, March 1972, p. 36.

of the consultant, accepts his proposals without subjecting them to *critical review*.[30] (Emphasis supplied.)

Within this observation is contained the seed of a "test of review" by corporate directors, to ensure that significant consulting services offered by the CPA are provided as expected.

Other leading practitioners (Robert Trueblood and Robert Beyer) also became involved in the consulting issue. Trueblood championed a notion of "test of review" which was subsequently cited in the comments of Briloff. Trueblood noted that:

> The real test of the CPA's independence stems from the professional environment in which he works. All phases of his audit work, all phases of his tax work, and all phases of his management service activity are, if challenged, subject to review, examination, and criticism *by his fellow practitioners*. If the *test of the review* can be applied to the work of any CPA and if the individual CPA is willing to undergo the critical appraisal of his work by others, then it is difficult to raise serious questions of independence about the propriety of a combined auditing and management service activity.[31] (Emphasis supplied.)

Indeed, in calling for a "test of review" by his CPA peers, Trueblood provided a key element to the potential for a process to properly manage CPA professional independence—systematic review by reasonable persons capable of ascertaining the facts and drawing conclusions.

Beyer focused on the involvement of the consulting practitioner in the decision process, and he expressed concern that in massive consulting engagements the client may become too dependent on the CPA. "The more complex the problems, the greater the tendency . . . for the ultimate decision to be made by the one who has so thoroughly canvassed

[30]Thomas G. Higgins, "Professional Ethics: A Time for Reappraisal," *The Journal of Accountancy,* March 1962, p. 32.
[31]Trueblood, "Management Service Function," pp. 42–43.

and studied the problem," he said. His focus was on this gradualism rather than on unbridled consulting activity. His concern was that the overeager marketing of *administrative* consulting (as opposed to accounting or systems-based consulting) would lead to a situation in which the profession would find it difficult to explain or develop a soundly based scope of services.[32]

SUMMARY

The events described in this chapter suggest a few elements of insight from which to develop a blueprint for consulting independence, and they are very important ones.

1. There is a clear need not to overexpand services and thereby create public expectations which cannot be uniformly met by all CPAs in public practice.
2. There is a view that the type of consulting—*information* as compared with *administrative*—may affect concerns about independence.
3. There is a need to recognize that independence in fact and in appearance will continue to be a concern and must be continually a subject for instruction and case analysis.
4. There is a basis within the process of peer review for "a test of review" related to consulting to be set forth.
5. There is also a presumption that competence will be carefully developed and maintained and that educational programs will be appropriately identified and supported to afford a steady stream of highly trained entry-level persons.

CPAs in public practice have and will continue to provide consulting services. The issue is to resolve the limits of con-

[32]Robert Beyer, "Management Services—Time for Decision," *The Journal of Accountancy*, March 1965, p. 46.

sulting practice with full attention to the concept of audit independence so that in audits, the consulting clients' CPA and his or her firm's decision process is satisfactorily *managed* to protect the public interest.

During the 1960s and early 1970s, consulting services became even more fully identified with the public practice of CPAs. The MASBOKE study provided an educational policy guide and the involvement of key professional leaders in the initial articulation of the *Statements on Management Advisory Services* were important steps in putting together the process to *manage* CPA consulting.

As to the concept of independence, academics noted that several *meanings* could be attributed to the term, suggesting that confusion over the *meaning* of independence indeed could exist. One element, the "dual financial standard" of independence, was now resolved since the SEC and the AICPA held to the same limit with regard to an auditor's financial involvement in a client. But greater attention would have to be focused on matters involving individual CPAs as consultants and their service relationships and attitudes toward independence in general and audit independence in particular in order to fashion a notion upon which consulting self-regulation could develop from professional moral authority. It was becoming time to analyze the basis of the profession's essential social role and to relate it by way of the *meanings* of independence in general (integrity and objectivity as cited by Carey in the concluding words of Chapter 3) to the CPA in consulting practice. Such an effort would be made even more difficult and stressful due to the lack of clear conceptual or operating precedent. The issue would therefore remain, and become one of the more widely debated topics in the years to come.

6

Controversy
In Search of
An Issue

1977 TO 1984

Many years of history support the relationship of client and auditor and the rendering of consulting services. Such an approach enhances substantially the economic value of the audit, both by increasing audit outputs and enhancing efficiency.[1]

John C. Burton, 1980

[1]John C. Burton, "A Critical Look at Professionalism and Scope of Services," *The Journal of Accountancy,* April 1980, p. 56.

In the wake of the repercussions of Watergate, the political mood of the country changed. Activist congressional delegates on the House Subcommittee on Oversight and Investigations (the "Moss Committee") began a series of hearings on regulatory agencies, including the SEC, with the intention ultimately of addressing "corporate accountability."[2] The first hearings were held in the Spring of 1976, generating several volumes of testimony and investigative activity continuing through the "Citicorp" hearings in 1982.[3]

These hearings, which eventually involved both the House and the Senate (in the form of the "Metcalf Committee"), mark what observers term "the coming of age of the accounting profession" and were the origin of the expression, "the accounting establishment."[4] This term was the title of the Senate staff study document prepared as background for the 1977 hearings. The thrust of this document was evident from its very title, since it focused principally on the large national and multinational accounting firms (The Establishment) rather than directly on the profession itself, at least at first.

The CPA profession would emerge from this period with an entirely different structure of governance than when the period began. Some of the institutional modifications, such as the formation of the AICPA Division of the CPA firms, were a response to the need to develop controls over the practice of CPA *firms*, rather than over *individuals*, as in the past. This was in recognition of the fact that the CPA firm had become a focal point in the economic environment. Other

[2]U.S. Congress, Senate, Hearings before the Subcommittee on Reports, Accounting and Management of the Committee on Governmental Affairs, *Accounting and Auditing Practices and Procedures*, 95th Cong., 1st sess., April 19, 21, May 10, 12, 24, 26, June 9 and 13, 1977, Washington D.C.: GPO, 1977.

[3]U.S. Congress, House, Hearings before the Subcommittee on Oversight and Investigations of the Committee on Energy and Commerce, *SEC and Citicorp*, 97th Cong., 2nd sess., September 13 and 17, 1982, Washington, D.C.: GPO, 1983.

[4]U.S. Congress, Senate, Staff Study by the Subcommittee on Reports, Accounting, and Management of the Committee on Governmental Operations, *The Accounting Establishment*, 95th Cong., 1st sess., Washington, D.C.: GPO, 1977.

actions, including the empowering by the AICPA of a public board (composed of distinguished individuals, including two former SEC commissioners) to act in oversight of the SEC Practice Section of the Division, may have preempted the investing of similar power in a governmental agency.

When the dust settled, a roll call taken, and the direction of the profession ascertained, it became clear that a major transition had occurred. The CPA profession had redirected itself, weathered a major challenge to its professionalism, and demonstrated the social justifications for its existence with sufficient strength to forestall any additional or amending legislation.

The profession, in its own behalf, had now to demonstrate that it could operate the machinery so swiftly installed that it would provide both the self-governance and the self-regulation expected by a dynamic and critical economic and political environment. It is not coincidence, then, that the scope of services for the profession and possible independence problems were principal issues at the hearings and in the design of the newly installed self-governance processes.

Never before had the profession been called on to reveal so much about its inner workings to so many who understood so little about the technical operations of accounting, auditing, and the process of satisfying SEC requirements. The educational nature of the hearings prompted one Senator to remark, at the conclusion, (CPA's should appreciate the understatement and irony) that: "This whole process has been such an educational process."[5]

This was not the profession's inaugural contact with Congress. Certainly in the Senate hearings of 1933 the legendary testimony of Colonel Arthur Carter, as president of the New York Society, is credited with influencing Congress to establish a role for CPAs in the audit provision of the Securities Act. Also, CPAs had periodically been members of major governmental commissions, providing testimony before

[5]U.S. Congress, Senate, 1977 Hearings, p. 1692.

congressional hearings as needed. The big difference was that the mood of the Congress with respect to CPAs had not been as aggressive—or as hostile. During the Moss-Metcalf hearings there was a judgmental tone underlying the attitude toward the CPA profession, which was captured in the title of the staff study itself.

CPAs immediately were placed in the position of having to defend themselves, given the testimony of the initial witnesses selected by the committees. The agenda seemed designed to cast CPAs not as publicly oriented professionals but rather as highly paid "flexible thinkers," used by managements of major corporations to ensure the control by the latter over the resources under their care. The passage of the Foreign Corrupt Practices Act (1977), the Equity Funding scandal, and numerous post go-go era litigations had made the CPA profession a choice target for politicians seeking to be identified with a subject which could capture headlines and earn credit in the public mind. Corporate accountability and the CPA profession were "it."[6]

THE POLITICS OF INDEPENDENCE

The CPA was again in the middle. As one corporate executive explained:

> The objective of those exerting the pressure is simple. They want to undermine the existing system—to transfer the governance of corporations and the accounting profession from the private sector to the public sector. . . .[7]

---

[6]American Institute of Certified Public Accountants, Report of the Special Committee on Equity Funding, *The Adequacy of Auditing Standards and Procedures Currently Applied in the Examination of Financial Statements,* New York: AICPA, 1975.
[7]Thomas Murphy, "Address to Partners of Deloitte, Haskins + Sells at Annual Meeting," *The Week in Review,* September 15, 1978, p. 3.

If GMC Chairperson Thomas Murphy was right, the important questions were: Where would the attack be focused? What was the chink in the profession's armor? Where was it most vulnerable? What characteristics could be most easily impunged and at the same time be most difficult to defend? "Independence" was a most likely target.

If the CPA profession was being challenged as a means of changing the economic structure, and an attack was to be launched on auditor independence, the next question was in what area or areas this could be most easily pursued. Several candidates emerged, including alleged audit failures, accounting and audit standard-setting processes, and one issue which lay close to the issue of independence—*scope of services.* This was ideally suited as an abstract problem of intractable dimension, involving a professional's "state of mind."

Assuming this scenario to be credible, the answer then was obvious: attack the independence of the CPA as auditor, question his or her credibility as one operating in the public interest, and establish rather that CPAs work only for their self-interest and the interest of their clients. If independence fell suspect, all else would fall, for both the character and the reputation of the profession would be without value in the market investment system.

Murphy continued:

> If this line of thinking is carried through to its logical—perhaps illogical—conclusion then the only persons that will be considered truly independent will be those on a government payroll. If our critics' narrow definitions of such terms as independence prevail, then only the least experienced individuals will be allowed to govern our corporations and the accounting profession. . . .[8]

[8]Murphy, "Address to Partners," p. 3.

THE PROFESSION'S GOALS: "PREESTABLISHMENT"

In 1974, the CPA profession had reconfirmed its earlier blue-print (1961: *Where Are We Headed?*) to be broad gauged and committed to a scope of service consisting of accounting and auditing, tax, and consulting. The MAS market, according to *Business Week*, would reach $2.5 billion in 1979, and was expected to continue to grow at an annual rate of 20%.[9] The profession, as previously related, also had experienced phe-nomenal growth; the AICPA-admitted members would num-ber 200,000 by 1983 (Table 5). Big Eight firms that had counted partners in terms of dozens now counted by hundreds. The mushrooming growth of the profession had occurred to some observers much like urban sprawl after World War II—it had taken on a shape of its own without a complete mechanism to review operations, particularly in the area of consulting practices.

The profession had invested heavily in its consulting "product line," and had a strong traditional claim on certain accounting and systems-based services, where its recognized expertise provided a comparative advantage over non-CPA consultants. Furthermore, the market seemed receptive to more services by CPAs at all levels of practice, in part because of the quality of the services, and in part because of the perception that the CPA profession delivered what it was called on to deliver and could work with ingenuity to resolve difficult and unique problems. In short, competence.

But in its haste to deliver service the profession had not always operated smoothly or consistently. Services were being provided in a proactive fashion: CPAs often tried to deliver whatever the client needed, and the range of offerings ex-panded from tax and advisory (systems) services to executive search, plant layout, acquisition counseling, and beyond[10]— and all without clear communication to the general public or critics who expressed concern about the existence of quality

[9]"The Growth of MAS," *The Journal of Accountancy,* August 1979, p. 86.
[10]Coopers & Lybrand, *A Study of Nonaudit Services—Facts From Over 900 Companies,* New York: Coopers & Lybrand, 1979.

Table 5. Distribution of AICPA Membership: 1970 to 1984

	1970	1971	1972	1973	1974	1975	1976	1977	1978	1979	1980	1981	1982	1983	1984
AICPA Membership	75,381	79,736	87,652	95,415	103,863	112,494	121,947	131,300	140,158	49,314	161,319	173,900	188,706	201,764	218,855
Public accounting	61.6%	62.0%	60.5%	59.8%	60.0%	59.1%	58.5%	57.5%	57.6%	55.0%	54.1%	53.3%	52.5%	53.0%	51.5%
Business & industry	31.3	31.1	32.9	33.6	33.6	34.6	35.2	36.2	36.2	38.6	39.7	40.4	41.8	41.0	42.5
Education	3.3	3.2	3.1	3.1	3.0	2.9	2.9	2.8	2.8	3.0	2.9	2.8	2.5	2.7	2.7
Government	3.8	3.7	3.5	3.5	3.4	3.4	3.4	3.5	3.4	3.4	3.3	3.3	3.2	3.3	3.3
Membership in Public Practice	46,435	49,436	53,029	57,057	62,430	66,506	71,314	75,528	80,723	82,141	87,339	93,082	99,141	106,800	112,673
Employed by:															
Firms with one member	20.3%	20.2%	20.5%	20.9%	21.5%	22.1%	22.3%	22.1%	23.9%	23.5%	23.8%	21.8%	23.5%	22.4%	23.1%
Firms with 2 to 9 members	33.6	31.8	31.7	31.5	30.5	29.7	30.0	30.1	29.9	32.3	33.1	34.5	34.0	34.0	34.0
Firms with 10 or more members, except 25 largest firms	7.5	8.0	8.4	8.7	9.3	10.1	11.1	12.0	11.8	12.6	13.0	14.2	14.5	15.0	15.1
25 largest firms	38.6	40.0	39.4	38.9	38.7	38.1	36.6	35.8	34.4	31.6	30.1	29.5	28.0	28.4	27.8

Source: AICPA, New York.

controls and binding professional standards to ensure that conflicts were resolved in a manner consistent with the independence of the CPA as auditor, the role on which the foundation of the profession rested.

"Independence," wrote one major firm, "is the cornerstone of a public accounting firm's professional status and of its credibility in reporting on the examination of financial statements." Few, indeed, would quarrel with that view.[11]

The consulting practice of accounting firms had become sufficiently important by 1978 to earn a position for seven of the Big Eight on the *Consultants News* top 15 list. Soon the list would be headed by Arthur Andersen & Co. and dominated by the largest firms, much as predicted by Lynch in his Harvard study of 1959.[12]

Non-CPA consultant competitors, sensing a power struggle and the potential for an economic fallout, were active in seeking weaknesses in the CPAs' posture of independence and competence—alleging further that it was an "unfair" tie-in for audit firms to accept consulting engagements from audit clients. They suggested that it would be more equitable if the CPAs' actions were "restricted" (which CPAs interpreted as "regulated") in this sector of the market—with the consequent economic effect that those remaining would benefit from the realignment within.[13]

---

[11]Arthur Andersen & Co., *Our Independence as Auditors Is Not Affected by Other Services*, Chicago: Arthur Andersen & Co., 1979.

[12]Thomas C. Hayes, "Accountants Under Scrutiny," *The New York Times*, June 25, 1979, sec. D., p. 1.

[13]The American Academy of Actuaries, "Is an Accounting Firm Independent if It Provides Actuarial Services to an Audit Client?" *Journal of Pension Planning and Compliance*, January 1980, pp. 37–65. Alan Taylor, "Major Audit Firm Cited for Unethical Practices," *Computerworld*, October 30, 1978, p. 21. Bryan Wilkins, "Ethics of Big Eight Involvement in DP Services Debated," *Computerworld*, May 28, 1984, p. 19. Bill Laberis, "Adapso Split in Vote not to Sue Big Eight Firm," *Computerworld*, May 16, 1983, p. 14. Marcia Blumenthal, "Adapso Tables Action Against CPAs, IBM," *Computerworld*, November 15, 1982, p. 73. Marsha Johnston, "CPAs Say Consulting is Part of Their Job," *Management Information Systems Week*, April 4, 1984, Sec. II, p. 13. Janet Bamford, "Hard Fight Over Software," *Forbes*, April 9, 1984, pp. 84–85. Richard Shemtob, "Should Audit Firms Provide DP Services?," *Computerworld*, November 30, 1981, pp. 31 ff. Larry King, "2 of Big 8 and Adapso in Detente," *Information Systems News*, December 13, 1982, pp. 21 ff.

Having at the outset suggested a political motive for congressional interest in the CPA profession, its independence, and related issues of scope and range of services, it would be well to temper such a view with others. From the view of a person trading securities in the market and from the view of an individual requiring consulting services, the profession certainly seemed capable of delivering the necessary advice. What was not clear was how susceptible to influence a CPA firm/practitioner might be. Would a CPA shave a few points off a bad corporate score to keep a consulting client, or could the CPA auditor, as a corporate watchdog, be fed a juicy consulting bone and be taught not to bark? Critics implied that the worst could, and even did, happen.

The general response must finally rest on a satisfactory answer to this question: *What is done to form and enforce the character of the CPA?* True professionals strive for a "zero defect" performance in all respects, including that of maintaining balance and objectivity in the face of pressures to the contrary. Sensible persons will, of course, realize that this is not a zero defect world. Failures do indeed occur, individuals in certain times and circumstances are indeed unable to maintain their proper balance. Institutional mechanisms were now in process to redefine the practice of public accounting and to minimize the risk of failure.

RECONFIGURATION OF THE CPA PROFESSION

Former AICPA President Wallace Olson, in his book detailing the history of the Institute during the period of the congressional oversight hearings, points out that the first and only witness called by the House Committee during the initial hearings was a renowned critic of the profession, Professor Abraham Briloff.[14] Therefore, the profession was placed on the defensive, at least at the outset. At best it was able even-

---

[14]Wallace E. Olson, *The Accounting Profession; Years of Trial: 1969–1980,* New York: AICPA, 1982, p. 37.

tually to use the sessions to educate the Congress and its staff regarding the realities of the profession's operations and the limitations of the public reporting process. But reversing the momentum of the hearings required facts and carefully considered testimony, backed up by a willingness on the part of the profession's leaders to take action to avert further governmental involvement in the financial reporting process and governance related thereto.

What were the *facts* regarding independence and scope of services in the public accountant's world?

There were some sharply honed allegations, principally by Briloff, that public accountants were not independent as a consequence of their performing consulting services (the watchdog had taken the bone). Previous inquiries by AICPA committees led the committees to report that they found no evidence to support such allegations. Briloff retorted, "I cite the discernible conflicts at Yale Express, National Student Marketing, the Wall Street Back Office Mess, and Westec to refute the AICPA's repeated assertion that there have been no reported cases of conflict."[15]

The Commission on Auditors' Responsibilities (the "Cohen Commission," headed by former SEC chairman Manuel F. Cohen) reported that it had analyzed these instances and that, in the first three cases cited, the auditors obtained information that reflected unfavorably on audited or unaudited financial information issued by the companies while they (the auditors) were providing the other (consulting) services. It was determined by the commission, in reviewing Briloff's allegations, that the auditors did not use the information so obtained to produce added audit benefits. But even so, as the commission pointed out, this allegation does not support the notion that other services *weakened* the audit function.[16]

[15]George J. Benston, "The Market for Public Accounting Services: Demand, Supply and Regulation," *The Accounting Journal,* Winter 1979–80, p. 36.
[16]American Institute of Certified Public Accountants, *The Commission on Auditors' Responsibilities: Report, Conclusions, and Recommendations,* New York: AICPA, 1978, pp. 94 ff.

In fact, separate management of audit and consulting functions, as had been recommended by some critics to "preserve" independence, produces just this type of insulating effect. And yet, ironically, such separation was now being used as a point of criticism. Some wondered if it was equitable to expect that critics should be allowed to have it both ways.

The Westec case, the commission noted, did cause concern in that it was possible that the auditors' involvement in the company's merger and acquisition program could have reduced their ability to conduct an independent audit. The commission acknowledged that giving advice on accounting principles, as was done in the Westec case, "can conflict with the auditor's responsibilities."[17]

In conclusion, the Cohen Commission noted that:

> Except for the Westec case (where the potential for impairment did exist, but where none was demonstrated), the commission's research had not found instances in which an auditor's independence has been compromised by providing other services. Indeed, some of (our) research indicates that performing consulting services may improve the audit function and benefit users. If the empirical evidence were the only consideration, the commission's conclusion would be clear: the evidence does not support the theory. No prohibition of management services is warranted.[18]

In 1985, Briloff testified before the House Subcommittee on Oversight and Investigations chaired by Representative Dingell (D., Mich.) and continued to allege that the facts of Westec supported his charges that audit independence was compromised by the consulting services which were rendered.[19]

---

[17]AICPA, *The Commission on Auditors' Responsibilities*, p. 102.

[18]AICPA, *The Commission on Auditors' Responsibilities*, p. 103.

[19]Gary Klott, "Accounting Role Seen in Jeopardy," *The New York Times*, February 21, 1985, sec. D, p. 22. Abraham J. Briloff, "Plus ca change, plus c'est la meme chose," statement before U.S. Congress, House, Subcommittee on Oversight and Investigations of the Committee on Energy and Commerce (Draft), Bernard M. Baruch College, City University of New York, February 11, 1985.

While the Cohen Commission did not recommend a pro-hibition, it was not issuing a clean bill of health either. There was a significant and persistent minority view that consulting conflicts were a serious concern. This group's interest was sufficient to warrant action by the profession to address quality control in the firms and to strengthen its attention toward independence. The commission's concerns were addressed by rules established for the AICPA's SEC Practice Section of the Division for CPA firms which proscribed or limited services, such as psychological testing and executive recruiting.[20]

ESTABLISHING A PROFESSIONAL TEST OF REVIEW

The Public Oversight Board (POB) of the SEC Practice Section of the AICPA's Division for CPA firms also began to obtain information about the range of services in which section members were engaged, in order to assess the impact of such services on independence and to consider the skills such services required as compared with auditing and accounting services. After an exhaustive study, the POB published a report in 1979 rejecting the view expressed in the Metcalf (Senate) Subcommittee Report that auditors be prohibited from furnishing to audit clients any nonaudit services other than tax services and certain computer and systems analyses such as those necessary for improving internal control procedures of corporations.[21]

"Such a draconian measure," POB Chairperson McCloy wrote, "would not only deprive audit clients of services that they obviously deem valuable but also would cause a sub-

[20]American Institute of Certified Public Accountants, *Report of Progress: The Institute Acts on Recommendations for Improvements in the Profession,* New York: AICPA, 1978.
[21]American Institute of Certified Public Accountants, *Public Oversight Board Report: Scope of Services by CPA Firms,* New York: AICPA, 1979, p. 2.

stantial reduction in revenues for many CPA firms, especially the smaller ones." McCloy also noted that "audit committees and boards of directors should consider all of the factors mentioned in the report. . . ." The board recommended certain fee disclosures and safeguards regarding actuarial services, and agreed to proscription of certain executive recruiting services since they exhibited a strong likelihood of impairing independence. Overall, the board's considerations were directed by a pragmatism explained as follows:

> Independence in an absolute sense cannot be achieved. When evaluating whether certain services should be prohibited, it is necessary to consider the potential benefits derived from the service and balance them against the possible or apparent impairment to the auditor's objectivity.[22]

Later (in 1979) the Senate committee whose recommendations had been rejected by the POB again held hearings and called upon the POB to testify. POB Vice Chairperson Ray Garrett appeared before the panel, then chaired by Senator Eagleton of Missouri. On the matter of scope of services, Garrett noted:

> We specifically recommended that the scope of the SEC Practice Section peer review program be expanded to require a review of MAS engagements to test for compliance with applicable independence standards. The section's executive committee has adopted our recommendations and its peer review committee is in the process of developing appropriate tests.[23]

---

[22]"POB Issues Report on Scope of Services," *The Journal of Accountancy*, April 1979, p. 7.
[23]U.S. Congress, Senate, Hearings before the Subcommittee on Governmental Efficiency and The District of Columbia of the Committee on Governmental Affairs, *Oversight of the Accounting Profession*, 96th Cong., 1st sess., August 1 and 2, 1979, Washington, D.C.: GPO, 1979, p. 79.

The POB, therefore, had begun the process of putting into
place a "test of review" for consulting services.

The questioning of Garrett continued:

> Senator Eagleton: "Would you say that it is central to the
> accounting profession that it maintain at all times in the pub-
> lic's eye the appearance of complete independence?"
>
> Mr. Garrett: "I would like to say, yes—certainly, indepen-
> dence is terribly important—but I think it depends on how
> closely you analyze the situation. Perhaps it depends on what
> public you are talking about.
>
> "Utter purity of independence is not attainable and never
> will be. The most obvious exception, so to speak, is the fact
> that the audit client selects the auditor and pays the bill. . . .
> It has been accepted for, I think, very sound reasons. First of
> all, there is no better system. . . . And most of the other ap-
> paratus, ethical pressures, legal pressures and all the rest that
> are imposed upon auditors are designed to cause them to
> overcome whatever unpleasant temptation might come from
> the fact that the audit client pays the bill.
>
> "I think the same is true with respect to management ad-
> visory services. I think one could take an attitude of ritual
> purity with respect to them, as we tend to do with respect to
> direct financial interests; but I do not think it is totally rea-
> sonable to do so. For when you get to that point in your
> thinking, you begin to wonder, well, do we have to cater to
> the dirtiest mind in the world or do we try to draw some
> reasonable balance between the reasonableness of appearance
> and weigh it against the good that it does? That is what the
> board tried to do."[24]

SEC ACTIVITY, ASRs 250 AND 264—ATTEMPTS AT REGULATION OF CPA CONSULTING

The SEC also acted, in ASR 250, by requiring public companies to make certain disclosures in proxy materials about

---

[24]U.S. Congress, Senate, 1979 Hearings, p. 83.

fees for nonaudit services when they totaled 3 percent or more of audit fees. This requirement was withdrawn in 1981, along with the companion ASR 264, which contained the philosophy of the SEC underlying the disclosure requirement. These releases, the profession contended, had a "chilling effect" on the attractiveness of CPA consulting services and acted to distort the market for such services.

Withdrawing these releases, the *Wall Street Journal* reported, indicated that the SEC felt "private regulation could be permitted to operate versus government agencies in the area."[25]

THE MAGNITUDE OF NONAUDIT SERVICES

The so-called ASR 250 disclosures had, however, provided a useful, if brief, information legacy. Professor Scott Cowen, who provided an early study of over 4000 proxy statements filed for public companies from October 1978 through June 1979, disclosed that the average percentage of consulting fees to total audit fees was 8 percent (tax consulting fees were 10 percent).[26] Later, more comprehensive disclosures (involving nearly 9000 SEC companies) suggest that by 1984 the shift of services was more pronounced.

When it invoked the reporting requirements of ASR 250, the SEC also sought specific information about actuarial services, plant surveys, consulting on employment benefits and compensation surveys, public opinion polls, and psychological testing. Since several of these had been proscribed for SEC Practice Section members, which would have caused member firms to suspend any of their activities in these areas,

[25]Stan Crock, "SEC May Ease Rules on Nonaudit Work Provided by Accountants to Their Clients," *The Wall Street Journal*, August 19, 1981, p. 6. "SEC Initiates Moves to Boost Competition Between Consulting, Accounting Firms," *The Wall Street Journal*, August 21, 1981, p. 4.
[26]Scott S. Cowen, "Nonaudit Services: How Much is too Much?," *The Journal of Accountancy*, December 1980, p. 53.

it was to be expected that, as Cowen reported, these services were rarely if ever mentioned in proxy disclosures.[27]

In place of the disclosures required under ASR 250, the SEC indicated that it was satisfied with the information about nonaudit services which would be publicly available as a result of a revision of the membership provisions of the AICPA SEC Practice Section in 1977. Information about the consulting services provided to public companies by their auditors was also expected to be available to boards of directors.

PROFILES OF PRACTICE—SECPS DATA

Fiscal year 1983 data for major firms from SECPS (SEC Practice Section) sources indicate that, for Big Eight SEC clients, less than 10 percent report consulting fees larger than 25 percent of the audit fee. Only one of the Big Eight reported having a single SEC client whose consulting fees were greater than 100 percent of the audit fee for three years. (The latter suggests that major, nonrecurring, MAS engagements are not common.) The SECPS information also reveals that MAS revenue from SEC audit clients was less than 7 percent of SEC audit fees for all but one of the Big Eight firms (Arthur Andersen reported 18 percent) (Table 6).

The information also provided to SECPS included gross revenues and fees by service type as a percent of gross fees. On a comparative basis, consulting fees as a percentage of total gross firm fees had increased from a range of 5 percent to 19 percent in 1977, to a range of 11 percent to 28 percent in 1984.

With a few exceptions, the data for other major firms confirmed the gross fee consulting percentage increase phenomena which were reflected in the data on the Big Eight. De-

[27]Cowen, p. 53.

tailed SECPS statistics for several hundred smaller firms (more than 30 of which have SEC clients) indicate that nearly one-third realize less than 50 percent of their gross revenues from accounting and auditing services—meaning that *over one-half* of their revenue comes from tax and advisory services (Table 7).

The data suggest that a transformation of the CPA profession *has already taken place.* The questions which now become important are: (1) How much greater will nonattest fees (particularly consulting) become? How soon? (2) How should the CPA profession communicate this "new identity" to consumers, clients, educators, and government? (3) What is the best way to preserve independence and enhance professionalism over the triad of major services (audit, tax, and consulting) in the future?

THE PROFESSION'S IMAGE

In the period up to and through the mid-1970s, the profession had maintained a low profile when compared with the popular images of medicine and law promoted by Marcus Welby, "The Paper Chase," Perry Mason, and so on. Accounting, in part because of the inquisitor's image of the audit function, or the detail-oriented image of tax work, had a nonglamorous public image. Moreover, CPAs were more comfortable not being in the public eye, with its accompanying controversy and political turmoil.

The Moss-Metcalf publicity marked the beginning of the end of that era. A new image was needed because a new identity had evolved—based on the practice which was now formed. Further, as creative efforts to market services were launched in the wake of revoking the ban against CPA advertising, more attention was being paid to the public image of the profession. At the same time, competition had created for some a "commodity mentality" regarding the audit

Table 6. Average Fee Distribution of Eight Largest AICPA SEC Practice Section Member Firms: 1977 to 1984

Firm	Service	1984 (%)	1983 (%)	1982 (%)	1981 (%)	1980 (%)	1979 (%)	1978 (%)	1977 (%)
Arthur Andersen	Audit	50	51	52	53	55	57	59	62
	Tax	22	22	21	20	20	20	20	19
	MAS	28	27	27	27	25	23	21	19
Coopers & Lybrand	Audit	66	66	66	67	68	68	68	68
	Tax	21	21	20	19	19	19	19	18
	MAS	13	13	14	14	11	11	11	12
	Other					3	3	3	3
Deloitte Haskins & Sells	Audit	68	71	73	75	76	78	79	79
	Tax	21	20	19	18	17	16	16	16
	MAS	11	9	8	7	7	6	5	5
Ernst & Whinney	Audit	62	64	65	67	69	71	72	72
	Tax	21	20	20	19	17	16	16	16
	MAS	17	16	15	14	14	13	12	12
Peat Marwick Mitchell	Audit	58	58	59	61	63	59	60	61
	Tax	25	26	25	24	23	20	20	20
	MAS	17	16	16	16	14	12	12	11
	Other						9	8	8

Price Waterhouse	Audit	65	65	67	68	72	74	77	77
	Tax	21	22	21	21	19	18	16	16
	MAS	14	13	12	11	10	9	7	7
Touche Ross	Audit	63	64	64	66	66	68	69	68
	Tax	23	23	23	21	20	18	17	18
	MAS	14	13	13	13	14	14	14	14
Arthur Young	Audit	61	63	64	66	66	67	67	70
	Tax	25	25	24	21	21	20	20	19
	MAS	14	12	12	13	13	13	13	11
Average	Audit	62	63	64	65	67	68	69	70
	Tax	22	22	22	20	19	18	18	18
	MAS	16	15	15	14	13	13	12	11
	Other					1	1	1	1

Sources: AICPA SEC Practice Section Annual Data. John C. Burton and Patricia Fairfield, "Auditing Evolution in a Changing Environment," *Auditing*, Winter 1982, p. 5.

Table 7. Average Fee Distribution of AICPA SEC Practice Section Member Firms by Tiers: 1983

	Firms	Accounting & Auditing	Consulting	Tax	SEC Clients
First Tier (A)	8	63%	15%	22%	8,787
Second Tier (B)	9	67	7	27	1,029
Third Tier (C)[a]					
Firms with SEC clients	185	59	9	33	643
Firms with no SEC clients	240	54	11	35	0
Third Tier Total	425	56%	10%	34%	643

	Accounting & Auditing Fees Less than 50%	Accounting & Auditing Fees 50% or More	Total
Firms with SEC clients	42	143	185
Firms with no SEC clients	84	156	240
Total	126	299	425

(A) First Tier Firms:	(B) Second Tier Firms:	(C) Third Tier Firms:
Arthur Andersen	Alexander Grant	All members of AICPA
Coopers & Lybrand	A.M. Pullen	SEC Practice Section
Deloitte Haskins & Sells	Fox & Co.	except those in First
Ernst & Whinney	Kenneth Leventhal	and Second Tiers.
Peat Marwick Mitchell	Laventhol & Horwath	
Price Waterhouse	Main Hurdman	
Touche Ross	McGladrey Hendrickson	
Arthur Young	Pannell, Kerr, Forster	
	Seidman & Seidman	

[a]Distribution of Accounting & Auditing Fees for Third Tier Firms.

Source: AICPA SEC Practice Section Annual Data.

function. The relatively fixed and mature nature of the market for audits offered little opportunity for expansion. Computer and data base technology, and the shifting of audit dollars into internal auditing in response to the 1977 enactment of the Foreign Corrupt Practices Act (see Table 8), seemed to spell a declining opportunity for long-term substantial fee income increases necessary to attract, challenge, retain, and compensate high-quality talent. The added fee-cutting pressure of competition for audits caused critics to remark that a dangerous temptation was being set in motion—that, as fees dropped, the incentive to apply proper levels of resources would be reduced in favor of retaining favorable profit margins; or worse, audits would be simply the "gimmick" or loss leader thrown in to secure more lucrative consulting contracts.

These new insinuations drew emotional retorts from CPA auditors, who viewed themselves as sufficiently professional to resist such threats to audit quality. Enormous investments in time and money were being made to improve and make more efficient the audit process. That, in the firms' view, was the response being made to competition.

THE PUBLIC'S OPINION

Public confidence polls commissioned by major CPA firms usually placed CPAs high, if not at the very top, of the list of professionals in whom financial executives, clients, or the general public placed confidence.[28] Polls commissioned by Peat Marwick Mitchell, Arthur Andersen, and Deloitte, Haskins & Sells all continued to indicate that the public and key

---

[28]Deloitte, Haskins + Sells, *An Opinion Study of the Public Accounting Profession,* New York: Deloitte, Haskins + Sells, 1978, pp. 2–3. Deloitte, Haskins + Sells, "The Perception of the Public Accounting Profession," *The Week in Review,* May 1, 1978, pp. 6–7.

Table 8. Average Dollar Expenditures on External Audit Fees per Million Dollars of Revenue: 1974 to 1984

Year	Manufacturing	Oil/Mining	Financial	Insurance & Utility[a]	Retail/ Service	Total	Average
1974	$630	$642	$1482	$306	$429	$3488	$698
1977	567	585	1335	291	373	3150	630
1978	586	712	1263	292	361	3214	643
1981	497	487	1549	288	311	3133	627
1982	517	477	1467	283	301	3045	609
1983	499	416	1160	250	280	2605	521
1984	480	408	1007	243	268	2405	481

[a]Average expenditures for Insurance and Utilities combined by averaging.

Source: R. Mautz, P. Tiessen, and R. Colson, *Internal Auditing: Directions and Opportunities*, Institute of Internal Auditors, 1984, Table C-5.

business community members were satisfied.[29] But a crisis in confidence existed in particular circles that had experienced the fallout of the banks and business failures during the early 1980s. For instance, among security analysts, portfolio managers, regulatory officials, and educators, one recent survey indicates there is a clear concern that independent accounting firms give in too easily to client pressure.[30] The collapse of ESM Government Securities in early 1985, capped by unprecedented widespread allegations that an external audit firm partner had accepted favors, were accented by the protestations of financier Marvin Warner, principal investor in a failed savings bank, whose own actions were under question. In defense of his reputation a March 1985 television news report (perhaps somewhat tongue in cheek) quoted Warner as protesting: "I never made a dishonest dollar in my life. It's all the accountants' fault."

Each newly announced lawsuit against accounting firms seemed to outdo preceding ones in the specification of damages; $40 million, $100 million, $200 million, $400 million. The increases seemed to have no end. Does this flurry of suits bear out critics whose allegations now cast doubts about audit quality and consulting service tie-ins? Do they reflect an increased market insurance cost in a competitive structure for audit services set in place in the 1970s which has formed a competitive economic environment and placed the quality of audit services which can be provided at risk? Or do they simply reflect an unfortunate result of what has been referred to as our "litigious society?"

[29]Research Strategies Corporation working with Opinion Research Corporation, *Independent Auditors as Appraised by Corporate Executive and Eight Other Groups*, a study for Peat, Marwick, Mitchell & Co., January 1984, p. A28. Opinion Research Corporation and Research Strategies Corporation, *Independent Auditors: How the Profession is Viewed by Those it Serves*, New York: Peat, Marwick, Mitchell & Co., 1983. "U.S. Business: Trends that Shape the Future," *U.S. News & World Report*, July 16, 1984, p. 102.
[30]Research Strategies Corporation, *Independent Auditors*, p. A28.

INDEPENDENCE AND ACADEMIC RESEARCH

Speaking in 1978, Professor John Shank suggested that the controversy over independence consisted of accusations in search of an issue. Shank concluded that formal, scholarly evidence about independence was sparse. He noted:

> Perhaps this is because the subject cannot be definitively researched. Like "materiality" or "relevance" it may be a perennial will-o-wisp which continually eludes our ability to circumscribe it. . . . on the other hand my inability to define a program of research to "lay out" the independence issue may be solely a function of infirmities. . . . If independence is a definable, researchable, resolvable issue, its resolution has so far eluded the world at large, as well as this author.[31]

OPTIONS FOR ACTION

Formal AICPA ethics actions as to the conduct and administration of consulting engagements, in particular with regard to selection and supervision of subcontractors and specialists, had been the object of two rulings in 1977. Each ruling had stressed the need for the CPA who supervised or employed a non-CPA to attain assurance of the professional integrity and reputation of the subcontractor party—and to be in a position to supervise and evaluate the work of employees who were specialists. These rulings, it seemed, confirmed the traditional expectations of CPAs who involved themselves with others.[32]

Shortly thereafter, an interpretation of Statement on Auditing Standards No. 22 (Planning and Supervision, para.

---

[31]John K. Shank, "Independence: Accusations in Search of an Issue," *"The Accounting Establishment" in Perspective,* proceedings of the Arthur Young Professors' Roundtable, 1978, Chicago: Arthur Young & Company, 1979, p. 64.

[32]"New AICPA Ethics Rulings," *The Journal of Accountancy,* May 1977, p. 111.

4(b)) set forth a position regarding the relationship between the auditor and the firm's personnel involved in undertaking nonaudit services to the client entity. In part, the interpretation stated:

> The auditor should consider the nature of non-audit services that have been performed. . . . If the auditor decides that the performance of the non-audit services or the information likely to have been gained from it may have implications for his examination, he should discuss the matter with personnel who rendered the services and consider how the expected conduct and scope of his examination may be affected. . . .[33]

In November 1979, Price Waterhouse proposed what it considered to be a positive alternative to resolve the deadlock over consulting services. Quoting the PW chairperson, Joseph Connor:

> We suggested that the SEC Practice Section of the . . . AICPA should promulgate guidelines that make clear that the development of information systems for audit clients, as well as marshalling and analyzing specific information for management decisions with respect to economic alternatives, are permissible areas of activity and raise no independence issues.[34]

This initiative was never concluded, in part because the profession instead chose to seek rescission of ASRs 250 and 264 (which occurred in 1981), and to inaugurate a third generation series of self-regulatory pronouncements, replacing the *Statements on Management Advisory Services* standards which did not formally obligate members under the AICPA Code of Professional Ethics. That booklet was a second-generation document based on the three first-generation state-

---

[33]"SAS No. 22: Planning and Supervision," *The Journal of Accountancy*, February 1980, p. 108.
[34]Price Waterhouse & Co., *Breaking the Deadlock Over Management Advisory Services: The Price Waterhouse Proposal for a Positive Alternative*, New York: Price Waterhouse & Co., 1979, p. 1.

ments on Management Advisory Services which had been issued in 1969.

The first current standard in the new series was issued in December 1981 following the withdrawal of ASRs 250 and 264. Under this arrangement, professional self-regulation was put in place to substitute for governmental/SEC regulation. Three standards have been issued in this area which concern:

1. Definitions and Standards for MAS Practice (December 1981)
2. MAS Engagements (November 1982)
3. MAS Consultations (November 1982)[35]

This series of statements is designed to specify, under rule 204 of the AICPA Rules of Conduct, standards deemed appropriate for management advisory services. An independence requirement is not specified in the new series. In the predecessor series, independence was cited as among "personal characteristics" in the first of eight standards.

THE "FACT" OF CONSULTING SERVICES

Thus, although the first two generations of CPA consulting standards made reference to independence, the third generation is distinctive and does not. The emphasis instead falls on competence and fulfilling a role as an "objective advisor." This view reflects the focus of the AICPA Committee on Scope and Structure (1975) which stated: "In performing these services, the profession must . . . observe certain constraints—primarily competence, integrity and objectivity."[36]

[35]American Institute of Certified Public Accountants, *Statements on Standards for Management Advisory Services,* New York: AICPA, 1981.
[36]American Institute of Certified Public Accountants, *Final Report of the Committee on Scope and Structure,* New York: AICPA, 1975, p. 3.

The view of those supporting "distinction" was the *fact* that consulting services were inherently different than auditing services, since a third party relationship was not maintained in consulting—thus the need for a distinction in the standards.

It is also noted in *Statement on Standards for Management Advisory Services No. 2* that: "In performing an MAS engagement, the practitioner should not assume the role of management." This sentence is supplemented by a footnote which reads:

> An Institute member or his employee might at times serve in the role of management for a client. The [statements] do not apply to situations in which the member or his employee serve in that role, but under rule 101 of the AICPA Rules of Conduct and Statement on Standards for Accounting and Review Services No. 1, independence might be impaired for purpose of an audit, review, or compilation of financial statements.[37]

The policy direction of this footnote and the third generation of MAS statements is more permissive with regard to client employment than any previous actions by the CPA profession. The specific omission regarding independence suggests that practitioners perceived that difficulties would exist in current consulting practice in attempting to make an independence standard effective. If CPAs' consulting standards differ from those which traditionally emphasize the public-practicing CPAs' independence, will the public understand and accept the reasons for the differentiation? This emerging version of a "dual" independence posture (between the audit and consulting functions) must be addressed by the profession's leadership. However, it is well to consider it in the light of the history of independence in the profession. A "dual"

[37]American Institute of Certified Public Accountants, Statements on Management Advisory Services No. 2: *Competence in Management Advisory Services*, reprinted in *The Journal of Accountancy*, April 1969, pp. 56–58. American Institute of Certified Public Accountants, *Statements on Standards for Management Advisory Services*, New York: AICPA, 1981.

direct financial interest standard regarding independence in auditing required three decades to resolve. Reconciliation there was among members of the same "cloth"—CPA auditors. Achieving a consensus as to the *meaning* of independence among consulting practitioners, many of whom may not be Institute members, may prove more difficult, but reconciliation is not impossible. What seems to be lacking currently is a viable proposal and a long-term commitment to such reconciliation. Current AICPA literature sets forth the following:

> All CPAs are required to maintain objectivity in performing their work. They are bound by a code of professional ethics to guard against subordinating their judgments to others. Further, in their role as independent auditors, CPAs cannot have a financial interest in a client's company or have certain relationships that might cast doubt on their objectivity.
>
> A consulting relationship does not impair an auditor's independence. A consultant does not act as a member of the client's management or as an employee. In fact, MAS can improve the performance of CPAs as auditors because it permits them to acquire a greater knowledge of client companies.[38]

A disturbing aspect of this new "distinctive" rationale contrasted to the traditional view is the possible fracture which it suggests in the heretofore monolithic (i.e., coherent and consistent) image of the CPA—particularly the CPA in public practice.

A MONOLITHIC VIEW

Such a monolithic view, simply stated, is that *a CPA is a CPA* (just as a lawyer is a lawyer), and the type of specialized service provided is a secondary consideration. Also, whether the CPA

[38]American Institute of Certified Public Accountants, "The CPA and Management Consulting," New York: AICPA, 1981.

is found in public practice, financial management, large practice units or small, or as an individual, the education, qualifications, and personal practice expectations should be consistent. Is this monolithic view appropriate for all CPAs? Should the *meaning* of independence reflect the differences in the roles which CPAs perform? Or as recently related by the AICPA Future Issues Committee: "Can independence and objectivity be maintained as the cornerstones of the practicing professional . . .?"[39]

How much change in CPA "character" will the public tolerate?

AN ENTITY MODEL

To focus on the issue of a monolithic CPA is a desirable but inconclusive approach. The individual CPA is but one part of the issue. The practice entity is the other. The monolithic prototype is achieved most clearly in training physicians for the practice of medicine, where the focus is on the development of the *individual.* Health care, however, also suggests another model for the future delivery of information services by the CPA, namely a group/firm prototype—*the hospital.* In such a model, CPA firms would accept responsibility for delivery of a broad range of services, drawing from the talents of several professional, paraprofessional, and clerical personnel, as is done in health care. The role of the CPA, like the role of the physician, would be central to such a model, but the gradient level of professionalism, the cost of service, and qualifications would be directed by market demand for each skill level.

To date, the CPA, particularly in the audit role, has been identified with the personal monolithic model. However, it

[39]American Institute of Certified Public Accountants, *Major Issues for the CPA Profession and the AICPA,* A Report by the AICPA Future Issues Committee, New York: AICPA, 1984, p. 23.

also would be useful to recognize that both models, the personal and the entity, could apply to the operations of the profession in the future. What is needed is a general perception that *both* apply, and a process of strategic planning to involve both in the future. Physicians direct health care; CPAs in the future can be expected to direct information services in an information-based society.

But the planning and orchestration of such a grand scheme of development seems to become lost in the confusion over administration of particular levels of service, such as consulting, and within those levels on particular issues, such as independence.

OTHER VIEWS

In a 1980 essay on the subject of independence, John C. Burton, former chief accountant of the SEC and a self-described "loving critic" of the profession, concludes that a positive program by the profession (e.g., to "manage" independence) is what is most needed to sustain the current approach to the relationship between independent auditing and non-attest services. Burton's view cited in the quotation at the beginning of the chapter was that many years of history support the role of the auditor furnishing consulting services. Cooperation in the audit process between the two, he points out, "is both efficient and more effective than confrontation."

In his view the matter of independence is of much less concern to those who are actively involved in the situation than to the general public and the unsophisticated user of CPA services. In fact, Burton has suggested that: "Rather than retrenching and limiting the scope of services, the profession could develop its role as an information systems resource for management. . . ."[40]

---

[40]John C. Burton and Patricia Fairfield, "Auditing Evolution in a Changing Environment," *Auditing*, Winter 1982, p. 12.

A new identity and image for the practicing CPA must incorporate the wisdom of Burton's suggestion, the experience of nearly a century of monolithic CPA existence, and the reality of the changed practice and service profile revealed in discussions and statistical information cited above. The following chapter should be considered with these strategic design factors as a backdrop.

7

After 1984:
A New CPA Identity

*By certifying the reports that . . . depict a corporation's financial
status, the independent auditor assumes a public responsibility
transcending away any employment relationship with [the] client.*[1]

**Chief Justice Warren Burger,
U.S. Supreme Court, 1984**

[1]Gary Klott, "Auditors Feel the Heat of a New Scrutiny," *The New York
Times,* May 13, 1984, sec. 3, p. 1 ff. "News-Lines," *U.S. News and World
Report,* April 2, 1984, p. 83. Stephen Wermiel, "Justices Allow Review
by IRS of Audit Papers," *The Wall Street Journal,* March 22, 1984, p.
2. Marvin J. Garbis, and Ronald B. Rubin, "Implications of the Sup[reme]
C[our]t.'s Holding of No Accountant's Privilege in Arthur Young,"
The Journal of Taxation, June 1984, pp. 342–45.

Chief Justice Burger's dictum was disturbing to many in the context of the case at hand, which involved a delicate question of the confidentiality of communications between an auditor and his client. Breach of this confidentiality, it was believed, would set up an adversarial relationship making difficult if not impossible the free flow of information so necessary to the conduct of an examination of financial statements. If auditors were to be viewed as inquisitors incapable of acting as impartial confidants, the examination would become, in the words of a witness at the 1849 hearings before the Select Committee of the House of Lords, "a mere technical audit."[2]

Yet, was not Burger's observation really a confirmation of what leaders of the accounting profession had been saying all along?[3] A contractual relationship between auditors and their clients does not transcend their ultimate duty to the "public," be that public composed of creditors, investors, or the financial community at large. Indeed, Justice Burger's words confirmed the social justification for the audit franchise and endorsed the profession's claim to it.

The expressed purpose of this study has been to identify factors influencing the profession of public accountancy's evolving services, to express some unifying themes in providing those services, and to suggest a proper place for CPA services in our system of private enterprise. A central function of the independent accountant in the United States is the examination of financial reports. However, as we have seen in Chapter 1, auditing was added to the list of existing services which underlie the historical practice of public accountancy. Recognizing attest functions as giving the contemporary CPA profession its character also implies an im-

[2]R.H. Parker, "The Development of the Accountancy Profession in Britain to 1919," University of Exeter, August 1984, p. 19.
[3]Paul Grady, *Written Contributions of Selected Accounting Practitioners*, vol. 2, ed. V.K. Zimmerman, Urbana, IL: Center for International Education and Research in Accounting, 1978, p. 65. John L. Carey, ed., "Independence," *The Journal of Accountancy*, December 1943, p. 458–59.

pact upon the other evolving services which CPAs are prepared to offer to their clients.

CHARACTERISTICS OF PUBLIC ACCOUNTING TODAY

Code of conduct amendments enacted in the last decade have changed the limits of identified and accepted professional behavior—for instance, CPAs no longer ban advertising, fee quotations, solicitation of new clients, and the like. Foreseeable and natural competitive forces are being used to assist practitioners as they address new challenges. Public accounting is more aggressive and proactive in seeking its markets than ever before. The crucial issue involves managing the change and preserving and enhancing the profession's esteem, adding credibility within the economic community.

Membership in the AICPA now is well over 200,000—not all of whom are in public practice, however (see Table 5, Chapter 6). Specialization and stratification seem to describe best the profile of the CPA profession that is emerging to meet the twenty-first century. Specialization is *both* by type of technical function and by industry, and stratification is by size of practice unit. The internationalization of business practice and investment, computer communication, and rapid transport suggest that added elements of complexity, both cultural and temporal, will make even more valuable the services of CPAs in an information-based economic environment.

A recent survey by an AICPA practice analysis task force reports that the mean age of CPAs in public practice is 39 years.[4] Although their practices are larger and more likely to be diversified, 13 percent of CPAs in national accounting firms devote *no* time to the audit function—as compared with over 25 percent in sole practice who spend no time in au-

---

[4]"AICPA Task Force Issues 'Milestone' Report on Practice Analysis," *The Journal of Accountancy,* April 1984, p. 9.

diting. These statistics are significant in that nearly half of
the CPAs in public practice work in local CPA firms. Most
CPAs devote some time to most of the 41 work activities listed
in the survey—over 50 percent of the respondents devote
time to 31 of the 41 activities. This principal finding indicates
that CPAs in public practice—in all types of practice units—
are similarly engaged in a multiservice profession. The
profession is unified in its diversity.[5] Thus, AICPA Chairman
Groves pointed out that small firms face many of the same
challenges as the national and international firms. Any differences are in degrees.[6]

The relative youthfulness of today's CPA and the ability
to serve multiple markets is evident from the study. This
suggests that the CPA profession is a strategic economic resource for the future as it was in periods of national economic
emergency, such as World War II. The role of all sizes of
practice units and their relationship to nonaudit services indicate that multiple service has been the form of practice for
decades and is clearly established. Currently, four of the Big
Eight accounting firms rank among the top 10 U.S. consulting firms:

1. **Arthur Andersen & Co.**
2. Booz, Allen & Hamilton
3. McKinsey & Co., Inc.
4. Arthur D. Little Inc.
5. William M. Mercer Inc.
6. Towers, Perrin, Forster & Crosby, Inc.
7. **Peat Marwick**
8. **Ernst & Whinney**
9. **Coopers & Lybrand**
10. American Management Systems[7]

[5]"AICPA Task Force Issues 'Milestone' Report on Practice Analysis," p. 10.
[6]"Profile," *The Journal of Accountancy*, December 1984, pp. 74–76.
[7]*Consultants News*, October, 1983, p. 4.

The list also includes five other major public accounting firms in the following order: No. 13—Price Waterhouse, No. 17—Touche Ross, No. 18—Arthur Young, No. 23—Deloitte, Haskins & Sells, and No. 25—Laventhol & Horwath.

ELEMENTS OF A PROFESSION

Public accountants identify their vocation as a profession and indeed it has been so recognized. Nevertheless, given the diversity of practice and the ever present need to reconcile those diversities with core attest functions, it is useful to trace some unifying characteristics or elements that go to make it up. No one of these elements is, by itself, sufficient. Some (save only independence, however defined) may be less important than others; most can apply to other "professions" as well, and many are characteristic of highly principled individuals who do not claim to be professionals. Taken together, they may describe by exclusion the present logical limits of public accounting.

Because of the size and economic capabilities of large public accounting firms, specialists of all kinds can and are being employed to carry out a variety of tasks. Smaller firms or individual practitioners also may have or acquire particular skills, and may choose to exercise them in pursuit of professional goals. Given the historically broad arena in which the public accountant operates, the question, then, is what should be done and why. Several constructs are important:

Independence. As we have seen, definitions and concepts of independence have not always been consistent over time or in relationship to the various services performed by public accountants. Nevertheless, with attest functions constituting the core function of public accounting, independence is the essential characteristic of the public accountant and the imperative of the CPA professional and the services which are offered as a result.

Skill and Legality. Professionals do not undertake tasks for which they are unprepared, and, of course, should not undertake those which by law are reserved to others (for example, medicine). Still, skills can be acquired and laws changed if necessary in a dynamic society.

Professionalism. Many writers have outlined the characteristics they conceive of as reflecting this intangible. Most important might be a definable common body of knowledge, individuality (decisions are personal, not collective), ethical constraints (self-discipline), altruism (placing the well-being of others above self-interest), and judgment (decision making in the face of uncertainty).

Adaptability. There is an "image" of public accounting that can be changed abruptly only with the risk of losing identity. Public accountants do what people think they do. Diversification and expansion of services, therefore, must recognize the need to address change with a sense of control, purpose, and gradualism. In order to be acceptable, an evolving service must employ recognized skills appropriate to present services and not compromise those presently offered.

Another characteristic of professionalism is that it does not employ the practices of "commercialism." The boundaries are ill-defined, but must be considered. Many leaders intuitively recognize the difference, yet have trouble defining it. CPAs *acting in their professional capacity* should not sell used cars, for example. Some have suggested that the code of ethics be amended to separate and recognize "professional" and "commercial" activities and apply different rules to each. Such an explicit segregation of activities would be destructive of the image of professionalism since it would postulate that a professional firm could engage in nonprofessional activities. Further, it would do nothing to clarify decisions regarding scope of practice but would likely complicate them as firms worked to test definitions and determine which set of rules applied to particular circumstances.

LOOKING TO THE FUTURE—THE ROLE
OF INDEPENDENCE

A crucial challenge for the accounting professional in the future is to manage growth and manage scope of practice so as to acknowledge the primacy of attest responsibilities. Without the core, a firm may be profitable and provide a valuable service to the economic community, but it will be something other than legislatively sanctioned public accounting. It is essential therefore to focus on the management and definition of independence. What design for future CPA services will provide the best means to assist society? How will such a design address the relationship between audit/attest services, results-reporting of information systems, and other consulting services? How will these relationships relate to the meanings of independence and the perception which the non-CPA has about CPA professionalism?

A recently released AICPA report identified 134 matters of concern to the profession and focused on 14 issues which were deemed most important overall. These included issues such as expansion of services, competition, computerization, specialization, quality control, CPA qualifications, and others. The sheer magnitude of the issues identified in this report precludes its application in this study. However, one of the 14 issues identified by the task force falls within the bounds of our consideration. As the task force related it, "The issue is, Can independence and objectivity be maintained as the cornerstone of the practicing professional or should broader concepts be emphasized?"[8]

The attribute of independence, some feel, can be better understood by using other terms—but the traditional one has much to commend it in the face of the changing service roles and the changing identities which CPAs are developing in their quest for economic and social purpose. It is one of

[8]American Institute of Certified Public Accountants, *Major Issues for the CPA Profession and the AICPA,* A Report by the AICPA Future Issues Committee, New York: AICPA, October 1984, p. 23.

the identifying characteristics by which the public recognizes the role of the CPA. All professions must exhibit integrity and objectivity, but independence is the cornerstone of the CPA's public role. It has also been shown that early writers and contemporary writers over nearly a century and a half consider independence an attribute of the work of an accounting professional. Yet the *meaning* of independence in each of the CPA's service roles—auditor, tax advisor, and consultant—may be acquiring an emphasis peculiar to that role.

In 1979, Henry Gunders, Chairperson of the AICPA's MAS Executive Committee, speaking at the annual MAS Conference, remarked:

> When all is said and done, let us not lose sight of the fact that no profession can survive, much less thrive, without rendering services that are *in the public interest* and are delivered productively and at a high level of quality.[9] (Emphasis supplied.)

Rule 101 (Independence) of the AICPA Revised Code of Conduct does not apply to CPA MAS activities—as was discussed in the previous chapter. However, Rule 102 (Integrity and Objectivity) which requires that a member "not subordinate his judgment to others," does apply to CPAs in MAS practice.[10] This raises a question of policy. How does Rule 101 differ from 102? In essence or in semantics? It must be considered that the distinction has been carefully made by leaders of the CPA profession to reflect a different role which the CPA consultant performs *specifically*—there is no third party outside of the consultant-employer relationship who relies on the work of the CPA consultant in the same manner

[9]"Special Report—MAS Conference Features Practitioners' Forums," *The Journal of Accountancy*, November 1979, pp. 12–14.
[10]American Institute of Certified Public Accountants, *AICPA Professional Standards (vol. B): Accounting and Review Services, Ethics Bylaws, International Accounting, International Auditing, Management Advisory Services, Quality Control, Tax Practice*, sec. ET 102.01, Chicago: Commerce Clearing House, June 1, 1984, p. 4421.

in which the investor relies upon the CPA fulfilling the attest role.

Several issues remain, however, even given the tenets of this position. First, will the public become confused by the subtle but important distinctions which CPAs make in defining their responsibility? By firmly eliminating references to an independence requirement, is the scope of potential SEC regulation of CPA services complicated? Do CPA consultants of a publicly held corporation incur any societal obligation, or is their exposure for deficiency limited by privity of contract—as was the traditional view of the role of the CPA performing attest services before *Ultramares*? Is a general use of a monolithic independence concept for the CPA profession, further defined by the specific service role of the CPA, feasible? Desirable? What social expectations are most likely to condition the role of the CPA in the future?

ELEMENTS OF THE CONTEMPORARY STRUCTURE

Membership requirements of the SEC Practice Section of the AICPA's Division for CPA firms include stipulations that members adhere to independence requirements in performing management advisory services (MAS) for audit clients whose securities are registered with the SEC, abide by certain restrictions on MAS work for SEC clients, and file certain information about MAS services with the Section, which becomes publicly available.[11]

There is, moreover, an emerging international expectation about independence. The November 1984 draft of the International Federation of Accountants on "Guidance on Incompatible and Inconsistent Businesses, Occupations or Activities" provides the following statement under the caption of "Independence": "When in public practice an accountant

---

[11]American Institute of Certified Public Accountants, *Division for CPA Firms SEC Practice Section Peer Review Manual,* New York: AICPA, 1981, p. 1–8.

should be and appear to be free of any interest which might be regarded, whatever its actual effect, as being incompatible with integrity and objectivity."[12]

For, as mentioned by GMC Chairperson Murphy in his analysis of the politics of independence quoted in a previous chapter, the role of the *independent* CPA in a free market system is considered vital to ensure the opportunity for such a system to operate and to withstand attacks by those seeking a more centrally controlled economy.

AUDIT COMMITTEES AND INDEPENDENCE

The business community, and public corporations in particular, by means of their boards of directors and audit committees, also are important groups to ensure that an "arm's-length" relationship is maintained between the CPA firm and management in all forms of service. As early as 1940, the SEC recommended the establishment of an audit committee composed of nonmanagement directors as a means of strengthening the independence of auditors. If this committee has a responsibility for the selection of the auditor and if the auditor reports to it and can refer disagreements with management to it, then the environment supports auditor independence.[13]

However, in 1978 a special AICPA committee stated that "we cannot conclude that audit committees are necessary either for the maintenance of auditor independence or for performance of an audit in accordance with generally accepted auditing standards." These comments no doubt will continue

[12]International Federation of Accountants, Ethics Committee, "Proposed Statement of Guidance on Incompatible and Inconsistent Businesses, Occupations or Activities," Exposure Draft, New York: International Federation of Accountants, November 1984.
[13]Deloitte, Haskins + Sells, "Auditor Independence," *The Week in Review*, December 8, 1978, p. 9. American Institute of Certified Public Accountants, *Report of the Special Committee on Audit Committees*, New York: AICPA, 1979.

to be challenged by critics of the profession. For the present, the requirements of the stock exchanges that listed companies have audit committees, and the voluntary actions of other entities in this respect, must be relied on to filter and weight independence issues, particularly as they relate to the performance of consulting services.

If, as has been held by Professors Burton and Shank, the issue of independence is intractable, or can best be satisfactorily resolved by reasonable individuals familiar with all the facts, have we not resolved the matter?

John L. Carey, whose career was attendant to matters of independence, concluded his active involvement by writing a paper, "The Independence Concept Revisited" (1970), and by commenting to the author several years later that: "The issue [of independence] was subject to being stirred up for self-serving reasons or by honest people who enjoyed abstract argument on insoluble problems."[14]

Can the book be closed? Probably not. Since independence is a principal value of the CPA profession, it is subject to public concern and scrutiny. Over time, as Carey's recent essay in the *Ohio CPA Journal* suggests, CPA independence has acquired its own specialized meaning, not entirely captured in the vernacular term "independence." If independence is to remain a viable concept, therefore, it will be amended and evolve in *meaning* as the demands of society change.

MANAGING SCOPE OF PRACTICE

CPAs are more than auditors. Indeed, their social responsibilities transcend the role of auditors for public corporations, although that role remains a principal public image. The perception of that role was reinforced by the U.S. Supreme Court decision quoted at the beginning of this chapter.

[14]John L. Carey, Letter to Gary John Previts, October 20, 1984.

Should the right to choose a CPA for more than audit work be limited by law or decided by the user of services? When does a real or imagined conflict of interest compromise auditor judgment and integrity? Do concerns about the perception of independence provide an adequate basis for replacing the marketplace in assigning CPA skills? Is it economically reasonable and socially equitable to deprive skilled and capable CPAs of the opportunity to provide a needed service, and to earn a living from their skills, if appropriate societal, professional, and firm safeguards are in place and functioning?

Consider the elements of the existing process. On behalf of society, state licensing boards assess skills, test those skills, grant licenses, and, most importantly, monitor performance and penalize transgressors—to the point of removing their licenses where necessary. The National Association of State Boards of Accountancy (NASBA) is starting to take an important part in coordinating these activities and in checking and validating the effectiveness and propriety of the licensing examination and the procedures surrounding it. At the federal level, SEC oversight and enforcement activities provide further review of public companies.

On behalf of the profession, the institutional safeguards include the Rules of Professional Conduct, the Joint Ethics Enforcement Program (administered by the AICPA with the cooperation of State CPA Societies), and the AICPA Division for CPA firms with its mandatory peer reviews, fee revenue reporting requirements, certain limitations on services, the Public Oversight Board, and the Special Investigations Committee which considers the quality control for member firms in view of alleged audit failures involving public entities. Individual practitioners and firms are thereby obliged to institute and follow internal methods of quality control that, in turn, will be assessed in the peer reviews.

In evaluating these "safeguards," the place of litigation should not be overlooked. The courts have been an important factor in defining the legal obligations of independent accountants and have not drawn back from defining CPA responsibilities and duties in particular circumstances. Pronouncements of the senior technical committees of the AICPA have been influenced by the result of judicial determinations. The desire to avoid litigation, with its potential for monetary and other penalties, including adverse publicity, has caused individual firms and the profession at large to devote enormous amounts of time and money to increase the amount of insurance for malpractice and to upgrade the quality of practice.

Early literature suggested that in the United States, at least, CPAs identified a natural market for their services as existing between the limits of the practice of law on one hand and the practice of engineering on the other. Such a model for a scope of services may still have appeal today, but with recognition that other groups of specialists seeking professional status, such as actuaries, now offer services in some areas (i.e., pension advice).

One difficulty with such a generalized (law-engineering) model, of course, is that international firms, as they expand services in other countries, encounter traditions which confound our provincial experience. For instance, in the United Kingdom, the traditional limits of accountancy are different when bankruptcy and receivership practice are considered. An amendment to the law-engineering model might also be necessary to recognize the strategic role which the accounting profession has indeed played internationally. In developing countries, for example, a firm can be the one to introduce new forms of technology—technology of all kinds, not necessarily related to accounting or advisory services as we recognize them in the United States—thus bridging the gap between advanced and developing countries.

The question of what is the appropriate *range* of services within the scope of consulting is more problematic. Early in the nineteenth century, as noted in the first chapter, which related experiences of the U.K. profession, this issue tended to defy a consensus. Attempts to unify the various city-based professional organizations were frustrated by an inability to achieve unanimity as to a description of what properly should constitute an accountant's practice. The dynamic nature of the markets serviced by accountants then and now tends to suggest that this difficulty—to complete and finally define a scope of services—will continue.

Duane Kullberg, chief executive officer of Arthur Andersen's worldwide practice, notes: "Some of this expansion [in range of consulting services] has been positive while other new services don't seem to fit as well within the image of a professional services organization."[15]

THE DANGERS OF COMPETITION

George Bernard Shaw is credited with an observation to the effect that: "Professions are but a conspiracy against the laity." Among other things, however, Shaw's comment illustrates the need for the CPA to seek an acceptable social balance between audit fees, competition, and professional independence. Where moral imperatives exist, as in the case of public accounting, open competition without the leavening of a strong sense of public responsibility is as apt to bring out the worst as it is the best of practice. This is often asserted by the profession's critics, who say that competition for consulting engagements has led to the treatment of the audit as a "commodity" for sale as a loss leader, or, worse, has led to a diminishment in audit quality to maintain profit margins. These allegations imply that "below cost" auditing cannot be in the public interest.

In studying matters related to this issue, Professor Shockley's research, published in 1981, pointed out that "among . . . the factors deemed to have a significant impact on the

[15]Duane Kullberg, "Kullberg: Play to Strength," *International Accounting Bulletin*, April 1984, p. 17.

perception of independence, competition was ranked most important."[16] A relevant point therefore becomes whether there is a point at which competition begins to undermine independence.

A SEARCH FOR BALANCE

The search for a balance between scope of services and independence may therefore rest not only in establishing a range of acceptable advisory services which are within the competence of CPAs but also in the institutional process by which independence is "managed" within firms which provide a full scope of audit, tax, and consulting services. The matter revolves around whether we as a group of professionals have a sufficient degree of self-discipline to voluntarily circumscribe our self-interest in favor of the well-being of the society which we serve, placing independence above economic gain. Some believe this can best be done by separation of audit and consulting personnel and intrafirm reporting responsibilities; others believe such an organizational split is dangerous, since it may result in the isolation of important information, and, particularly in smaller organizations, in inefficient and impractical personnel usage and lack of professional challenge.

Competition and its effect on the relationships between auditing and the other services offered by public accounting firms is not the only factor to be considered. The market for advisory services is wide, and there are many other players on the field. In 1981, the AICPA took an important step to recognize the breadth of this market, proposing to expand the definition of "advisory services" to include "informal advice," such as consultations based on personal knowledge,

---

[16]Randolph A. Shockley, "Perceptions of Auditors' Independence: An Empirical Analysis," *The Accounting Review*, October 1981, p. 785.

done in a short time and usually communicated to the client orally.[17]

Competitors of public accountants speculated that this new definition, which would bring the smaller firms shoulder to shoulder with the major firms in defending CPA "rights" to consulting services, "could be a very clever and devious move by the CPA profession (i.e., the Big Eight) to guarantee continuation of lucrative MAS divisions."[18]

No comment could signal more clearly the economic concerns of non-CPA competitors about the strength of accounting firms to command attention in the marketplace. At the same time, any move made by the profession to institutionalize its strength in changing service markets would be challenged by others who would propose that economic self-interest was the principal motivating force of CPAs' actions.

DEVELOPING A NEW IMAGE

The vision of the future for some is of a vast and unfettered profession. The senior partner of one of the Big Eight in the United Kingdom was reported in the December 1983 issue of the *International Accounting Bulletin* to have asked, "What is the right description for a firm comprised of engineers, economists, actuaries, information technologists, as well as accountants?" He thereby challenged at least one of the initial limits of practice for accountants—that of engineering. Presumably he would not cavil at others. The *Bulletin*, in a questionnaire sent to selected managing partners of firms around the world, asked the question: "In the long term, how desirable is a 'superfirm' of professional advisors—offering companies a full range of advisory services and perhaps combin-

[17]"Accountants Widen Scope of Recognized Management Advisory Services," *Consultants News*, May 1981.
[18]*Ibid.*

ing firms of accountants with lawyers, consultants, etc.?" The publication thus challenged the other boundary—that of law.[19]

To suggest a conversion of CPA firms into consulting firms of such breadth, in the near term at least, would seem to run an unacceptable risk of loss of identification. An amalgam of personnel—engineers, economists, actuaries, information technologists, as well as CPAs—would be brought together, with little initial prospect of developing a professional identity. Without that identity, such a firm might literally be unmanageable—and unable to perform up to the expectations of society and its own profession's moral imperative.

Clearly, public accountants can elect to continue to meet their core attest duties as to financial reports and at the same time strengthen their identity in the field of taxation, and as consultants. The latter is already being done; witness the rankings achieved by accountants in the consultant "top 10" list cited earlier. But will this resolve the matter? It does indeed suggest an evolutionary alternative, since it is already on track.

However, (1) the development of some reasonable definition of an appropriate range of consulting practice must go forward within the profession—among all firms, not just the large ones, and (2) self-regulation and the "test of review" within the profession must be perceived to be effective. The years since the Moss-Metcalf congressional hearings in the late 1970s have seen great strides in the latter; we have noted how difficult the former was to rationalize in the United Kingdom before the turn of the century. The jury is still out in this country, and failure by the profession to adequately manage independence inevitably will lead to constraints imposed from without.

To evolve in a rational manner requires some concept of what the new public image ought to be and it must be consistent with the CPA's new *identity*. Such a public image pref-

---

[19]"Diversification and Professional Structures: Views From the Top," *International Accounting Bulletin*, March 1984, pp. 10–14.

erably should build on and retain the present heritage of the CPA profession and consolidate the triad base of public practices consistent with concepts of self-regulation and the test of review. The elements of a profession must be present.

An institutional model (the hospital) was described earlier as a means of serving to manage more effectively a diversity of services as the public practice of the CPA profession evolves. Such a model relies on physicians and other health care professionals with a common body of knowledge, training, and moral commitment to manage and control various levels of talent carrying out a number of different services—all in the ultimate interest of the client (patient). Whether such a model is explicitly adopted or not, it offers a useful and possibly fruitful way to think about the future of the CPA profession.

THE CPA OF TODAY

The practitioners of the profession of public accounting— the CPAs offering services to their clients in a free enterprise economy—are not the only members of that profession. A broader perspective recognizes the interests and participation of many others, including CPAs in academe, in private employment (or outside of accounting entirely), and of those in government or other public service. All must contribute, and all have a contribution to make. Other individuals not directly a part of the profession, such as government regulators and clients themselves, also must participate in developing the identity and image of the public accounting profession.

MARKING A PATH

Some guideposts arising out of the material covered in this study may be useful as, collectively, the profession considers its future.

1. The notion that the CPA profession is bounded only by law and engineering in its service role. This is useful as a generalization, although it is not entirely practicable as a model in today's complex environment. This notion acknowledges the ability of the CPA to provide services in an information economy, but does not limit such services to results-reporting and attest duties as long as the profession also enforces the provision that an independent mental attitude is expected in *all* forms of service.

2. The view that the CPA profession is a strategic resource in the United States and a means of transferring information technology and results-reporting skills to other economies seeking the benefits of free enterprise. This "strategic resource" view would compel government officials and critics alike to consider the profession from yet another view. In an information society, the vital role of the CPA in the system of free enterprise would be recognized, monitored, and supported.

3. The recognition that independence will always be an issue. CPAs must continuously modify the concepts of peer review, management of quality control, and continuing education in order to ensure an informed compliance with the requirements of independence.

    Several commentators have noted that there is a "test of review" related to the attest function through the operations of the SEC, and by means of the IRS in terms of the tax advisory service, but that no similar "countervailing review" exists for advisory services to bolster independence. This comment, of course, ignores the role of peer review in those instances where such review considers independence, consulting engagements, and public audit clients and the role of the Public Oversight Board. These self-regulatory steps had no counterpart when attest and tax services were first introduced decades ago.

In an address entitled "Measuring Up to Our Maturity," Joseph E. Connor, Senior Partner of the U.S. practice of Price Waterhouse summed up the matter as follows:

> Let's consider the scope of services issue. I believe it is a credit to the AICPA, the Public Oversight Board and the individual firms that the SEC has decided to get out of the business of regulating in this area, as signified by its rescinding ASRs 250 and 264. It's now up to us to assure the SEC of our diligence in maintaining the fact and appearance of independence, even as we are called on to provide a broader range of services in a rapidly changing technological and economic environment. They must also be assured that our nonaudit services are subject to the same exacting standards as our audit services.[20]

4. The need for a basic commitment from accounting academicians to conduct research, investigate issues, and develop elements in educational programs at all levels which consider the duties and responsibilities inherent in the role of the independent CPA and the changing scope of publicly offered services. Such efforts would be useful in identifying literature, precedents, and issues related to professional duties and responsibilities of CPAs in a new practice environment of multiple services. They could also provide study opportunities, education, and public information about issues related to proposed CPA roles in specific cases.

5. The recognition that independence is best articulated as a moral or cultural imperative through a process of establishing a social expectation within the CPA profession. This expectation can be passed along as each individual is trained, first at the university level,

[20]Joseph E. Connor, "Measuring Up to Our Maturity," *The CPA Journal,* January 1983, p. 12.

next at the firm level, with the emphasis upon the individual's responsibility to regard independence as a *personal characteristic*. This view would by way of analogy regard independence in mental attitude as a matter of the CPA's *character*. Independence in appearance would be regarded as a matter of maintaining professional *reputation*. Thus the CPA would seek to maintain both in character and in reputation a mental attitude and an appearance of independence. This multilayered responsibility process would combat ignorance of independence responsibilities and aid in preventing innocent but nevertheless potentially harmful transgressions. Integrity would be an ongoing matter—for it is too important to be left to a game of checklists.

6. The awareness that society's expectations about the range of CPA consulting services must be based on the ability of the professional to achieve and maintain a general and uniform level of technical competence.

   Such technical competence should be commonly obtained as part of a professional program of preparation which requires prospective entrants to the profession to analyze and discuss matters of independence and accounting policy as an integral part of identifying issues. In this manner society will be able to distinguish CPA preparation from that of other accountants and business students. The practical effect of this awareness and preparation will be upon the formal education process—to include curricula, and, at the entry level, professional examination focusing upon a CPA's duties and responsibilities.

7. The necessity for corporations to participate effectively in performing a "market test" of services through effective involvement of board committees, such as the audit committee, in considering and selecting consulting services offered by all providers. Corporate in-

volvement in evaluating the degree and extent of non-attest services to be offered by a CPA firm which also provides attest services is a necessary element in a free enterprise system's operations. Effective audit committee action works to strengthen the reputation of CPA independence and to ensure proper service value in the marketplace.

Alternatively, there is academic support and informed professional opinion which suggests that added information an independent auditor acquires in performing advisory work can provide the basis for a higher quality audit. Thus advocates of draconian measures to limit CPAs from providing nonattest services to attest clients may play unwittingly into the hands of corporate management who seek to limit the effective knowledge of CPAs performing attest functions by deliberately "dividing" up the services and "conquering" the prospect of CPAs increasing their insights about client operations and relating effectively to board members on critical issues.

Board/audit committee involvement also helps address the claim by competitors seeking to discredit CPA consulting services that an "unfair advantage" inures to CPAs who have an attest contract. The active role of the board and its audit committee could evaluate any perceived merits to such concerns on a case-by-case basis.

8. The oversight role of government in the scope of services issues must be recognized. If the CPA profession fails to protect the public interest—due to improper or inadequate service, incomplete training, or improper safeguards as to its independence—then the government, through its appropriate agencies, must inquire and be prepared to set forth an agenda to remedy the demonstrated inadequacies.

9. The expectation that practice units will provide an appropriate system of training and review for entry level

professionals must be realized. This system would afford a sense of identification and personal responsibility for independence and competence. The CPA profession has, by direct right of state law, by federal law, and in the recent U.S. Supreme Court case law, been charged with protecting the public interest in matters relating to the attest function. Individual firms and practice units have a commensurate responsibility to instill these notions and to encourage professional employees to observe their compliance.

What will remain a point of debate, to be resolved with sufficient consensus to achieve public credibility, will be the matter of the appropriate range of advisory services. The attributes of the CPA profession which circumscribe the resolution of this debate are not absolute, but must involve an educational process which instills accounting-based technical competence, independence, and attention to judgmental skills on a broader scale than traditionally provided in a baccalaureate program of study. The resolution must also evoke personal commitments from CPAs to guard both the character and reputation of CPA independence and of professional institutions to provide credible processes of quality review.

CONCLUDING COMMENTS

The CPA profession in this century has provided countless opportunities for aspiring individuals to earn a better standard of living by responding to a career of responsibility which requires extensive educational preparation, testing, and review. Public accounting continues to be an open professional opportunity, for women, minorities, and all interested applicants.

A strong and developing CPA profession is essential to the preservation of free enterprise and to the success of small firms and entrepreneurial individuals who are the source of

future economic development and require the special advice
and services offered by trained CPAs.

Principal CPA firms have in many ways already become
much like "business hospitals," combining the specialized skills
of many related disciplines under the direction of individual
CPA professionals. The challenge now is to design, implement, and orchestrate the management of the institutions
and individuals composing the CPA profession in a manner
consistent with the expectations and needs of our society and
its economic system.

In the final analysis, accountants and historians writing of
our era from the perspective of times yet to come will evaluate
the quality of statesmanship and the wisdom of our leaders,
who are now required to bring about a resolution of the issues
before us. These relate importantly to the management of
independence and the relationship of attest to nonattest services offered by professionals calling themselves certified *public* accountants.

Recently Arthur M. Wood, chairman of the AICPA Public
Oversight Board, addressed the Institute's Council and observed:

> We are meeting here at what I believe is a critical time in the
> history of the accounting profession in this country. The cause
> of this crisis is the fact that investors and depositors are losing
> faith in the ability of the accounting profession to perform
> the job which has historically been its unique function in our
> society—assuring the integrity of the financial information
> upon which our capitalistic society necessarily depends.[21]

Writing in 1944, Victor Stempf, then president of the American Institute, noted the value of a timeless strategic quality
which relates to deliberations about our multiservice-based
CPA profession today, namely that:

[21] Arthur M. Wood, "POB Chairman Urges Major Changes in Self-Regulatory Program for Accountants," *DH&S Review*, May 27, 1985, p. 1.

Statesmanship in the profession looks beyond immediate selfish interest or expediency toward the long range development of the influence, recognition, and prestige of the profession through unmistakable service in the public interest. Statesmanship demands constant vigilance and vigorous action. . . . As a profession we have an inalienable right to set for ourselves objective standards of independence, integrity and competence.[22]

We could do no better than to follow his advice.

---

[22]Victor H. Stempf, "Report of the President of the American Institute of Accountants," *The Journal of Accountancy*, December 1944, p. 451.

Appendix:
Selected Research
Bibliography

ACADEME

Antle, Rick, "Auditor Independence," *Journal of Accounting Research,* Spring 1984, pp. 1–20.

Aram, John D., and Gary John Previts, "The Auditor and Management Relationships in the United States," *Accountants Record,* December 1980, pp. 20–22.

Bailey, Andrew D. Jr., R. Preston McAfee, and Andrew B. Whinston, "An Application of Complexity Theory to the Analysis of Internal Control Systems," *Auditing,* Summer 1981, pp. 34–37.

Boland, Richard Jr., "A Positive View of Management Advisory Services and the Public Well-Being," *The Ohio CPA Journal,* Summer 1983, pp. 139–43.

Briloff, Abraham J., "The Congressional Oversight of the Accounting Profession in the United States," statement to The Third International Congress of Accounting Historians, London, August 17, 1980.

Briloff, Abraham J., "The Odd Couple," Chapter 9 in *The Truth About Corporate Accounting,* New York: Harper & Row, 1981, pp. 148–69.

Chandler, Alfred D., "The Emergence of Managerial Capitalism," *Business History Review,* Winter 1984, pp. 473–503.

Davidson, Sidney, "The Day of Reckoning—Managerial Analysis and Accounting Theory," *Journal of Accounting Research,* Autumn 1963, pp. 117–26.

Goldman, Arieh, and Benzion Barlev, "The Auditor–Firm Conflict of Interests: Its Implications for Independence," *The Accounting Review,* October 1974, pp. 707–18.

Imhoff, Eugene A. Jr., "Employment Effects on Auditor Independence," *The Accounting Review,* October 1978, pp. 869–81.

Knapp, Michael Chris, "An Integrative Empirical Analysis of Auditor Independence," Ph. D. dissertation, University of Oklahoma, 1982.

Lacey, John M., "Issues in the Perception of Auditor Independence," SEC & Financial Reporting Institute, University of Southern California, April 1985.

Merino, Barbara Dubis, and Marilyn Dale Neimark, "Disclosure Regulation and Public Policy: A Sociohistorical Reappraisal," *Journal of Accounting and Public Policy,* Fall 1982, pp. 33–57.

Needles, Belverd E., ed., "The Emerging Practice of Accounting," proceedings of The DePaul University Research Symposium, 1982–83, DePaul University, Chicago, May 12 and 13, 1983.

Nichols, Donald R., and Kenneth H. Price, "The Auditor–Firm Conflict: An Analysis Using Concepts of Exchange Theory," *The Accounting Review,* April 1976, pp. 335–46.

Pany, Kurt and Philip M.J. Reckers, "The Effect of Gifts, Discounts, and Client Size on Perceived Auditor Independence," *The Accounting Review*, January 1980, pp. 50–61.

Pany, Kurt and P.M.J. Reckers, "Auditor Independence and Nonaudit Services: Director Views and Their Policy Implications," *Journal of Accounting and Public Policy*, Spring 1983, pp. 43–62.

Pearson, Michael A., "Categories of Independence: How Does Your Firm Measure Up?" *The Journal of Accountancy*, July 1980, pp. 39 ff.

Pearson, Michael A., "Enhancing Perceptions of Auditor Independence," *Journal of Business Ethics*, 4, 1985, pp. 53–56.

Ratliff, Richard L., "A Study of Selected Congressional Attitudes Regarding Public Accounting Issues," Ph. D. dissertation, University of North Carolina at Chapel Hill, 1979.

Reckers, Philip M.J., and A.J. Stagliano, "Non-Audit Services and Perceived Independence: Some New Evidence," *Auditing*, Summer 1981, pp. 23–33.

Scheiner, James H., and Jack E. Kiger, "An Empirical Investigation of Auditor Involvement in Non-Audit Services," *Journal of Accounting Research*, Autumn 1982, pp. 482–96.

Schulte, Arthur A. Jr., "Compatibility of Management Consulting and Auditing," *The Accounting Review*, July 1965, pp. 587–93.

Schulte, Arthur A. Jr., "Management Services: A Challenge to Audit Independence?" *The Accounting Review*, October 1966, pp. 721–28.

Simunic, Dan A., "Auditing, Consulting, and Auditor Independence," *Journal of Accounting Research*, Autumn 1984, pp. 679–702.

PRACTITIONERS

Chenok, Phillip B., "The Exciting Challenges of MAS," *The Journal of Accountancy*, June 1981, pp. 81–84.

Delves, Eugene L., "From the President," *ICPAS Newsjournal*, May 1984, p. 2.

Elliott, Merle S., and Monroe S. Kuttner, "MAS: Coming of Age; The Need For and Implications of the First MAS Standards," *The Journal of Accountancy*, December 1982, p. 66.

Flegm, Eugene H., *Accounting: How to Meet the Challenges of Relevance and Regulation*, New York: Wiley, 1984.

Klion, Stanley R., "MAS Practice: Are the Critics Justified?," *The Journal of Accountancy*, June 1978, pp. 72–78.

Mednick, Robert, "Call for New Standards of Attestation," *The CPA Journal*, August 1984, pp. 13–16.

Olson, Wallace E., "What is Auditor 'Independence'?" *The Journal of Accountancy*, April 1980, pp. 80–82.

GOVERNMENT PUBLICATIONS

U.S. Congress, Joint Committee Study For the Use of Subcommittee on Economic Growth and Stabilization of the Joint Economic Committee, *The Costs of Government Regulation of Business*, 95th Cong., 2nd sess., April 10, 1978, Washington, D.C.: GPO, 1978.

U.S. Congress, Senate, Prepared by the Securities and Exchange Commission for the Subcommittee on Governmental Efficiency and the District of Columbia of the Committee on Governmental Affairs, *Securities and Exchange Commission Report to Congress on the Accounting Profession and the Commission's Oversight Role*, 95th Cong., 2nd sess., July 1978, Washington, D.C.: GPO, 1978.

U.S. Congress, Senate, Prepared by the Securities and Exchange Commission for the Subcommittee on Governmental Efficiency and the District of Columbia of the Committee on Governmental Affairs, *Securities and Exchange Commission Report to Congress on the Accounting Profession and the Commission's Oversight Role*, 96th Cong., 1st sess., July 1979, Washington, D.C.: GPO, 1979.

Williams, Harold M., Chairman Securities and Exchange Commission, *Corporate Accountability and Corporate Power*, paper presented at the Fairless Lecture Series, Carnegie-Mellon University, Pittsburgh, October 24, 1979.

U.S. Congress, Senate, Prepared by the Securities and Exchange Commission for the Subcommittee on Governmental Efficiency and the District of Columbia of the Committee on Governmental Affairs, *Securities and Exchange Commission Report to Congress on the Accounting Profession and the Commission's Oversight Role*, 96th Cong., 2nd sess., August 1980, Washington, D.C.: GPO, 1980.

Index

Self-discipline, and auditing in United
    Kingdom, 13, 27–28
Sells, Elijah Watt, 41, 42, 49, 53
Shank, John, 143, 161
Sharaf, Hussein A., 81, 103
Shaw, George Bernard, 164
Shemtob, Richard, 126n
Shifflett, Everett, 89
Shockley, Randolph A., 164–165
Skill, as essential characteristic of
    public accountant, 156
Statement of Auditing Standards No.
    22, 143–144
*Statements on Management Advisory
    Services,* 113–114, 144–145, 146
Stempf, Victor, 174–175
Sterrett, Joseph, 37–38
Stockwell, Herbert G., 38–39
Summers, Edward L., 113n
Swieringa, R. J., 108

Tax consultants, role of CPAs as, 4, 5
Taylor, Alan, 126n
Telegraph Construction &
    Maintenance Co., Ltd., 25
Test of review, 104, 115–117,
    130–132, 167, 169
Titard, Pierre, 107, 112
Touche, Niven & Co., establishment of
    production cost department by,
    50
Touche Ross, 155
  average fee distribution of, 137
  development of management
    services at, 88
Towers, Perrin Forster & Crosby, 154
Trueblood, Robert, 104, 116

United Kingdom, development of
    public accountancy in, 11–31,
    39, 163
U.S. Steel Corp., employment of
    auditors by, 35

Veysey, William B., 49
Voluntary shareholder audits, 60

Wallace, Frank, 89
Wall Street Back Office Mess case, 128
Warner, Marvin, 142
Watts, Ross L., 17n
Wellington, Roger, 91n
Wellington Committee, 91
Welsch, Gemma M., 5n
Wermiel, Stephen, 151n
Werntz, William, 76
Westec case, 106, 128, 129
Whinney, Smith and Whinney, fee
    income schedule of, 22–25
Wiesen, Jeremy, 61n
Wilcox, Edward B., 96n
Wilensky, Harold L., 101n
Wilkins, Bryan, 126n
Williams, Harold, 100, 101
Wise, J. A., 89n
Wood, Arthur M., 174

Yale Express case, 128
Young, Arthur, & Co., 17, 51, 155
  average fee distribution of, 137
Younkins, Edward W., 42n

Zimmerman, Jerold L., 17n